Witchcraft...into the wilds

Witchcraft...into the wilds

Rachel Patterson

MOON
BOOKS

Winchester, UK
Washington, USA

First published by Moon Books, 2018
Moon Books is an imprint of John Hunt Publishing Ltd., Laurel House, Station Approach,
Alresford, Hants, SO24 9JH, UK
office1@jhpbooks.net
www.johnhuntpublishing.com
www.moon-books.net

For distributor details and how to order please visit the 'Ordering' section on our website.

ISBN: 978 1 78535 459 5
978 1 78535 460 1 (ebook)
Library of Congress Control Number: 2017936410

A CIP catalogue record for this book is available from the British Library.

Design: Stuart Davies

UK: Printed and bound by CPI Group (UK) Ltd, Croydon, CR0 4YY
US: Printed and bound by Thomson Shore, 7300 West Joy Road, Dexter, MI 48130

We operate a distinctive and ethical publishing philosophy in
all areas of our business, from our global network of authors to
production and worldwide distribution.

Contents

With huge thanks to my husband Peter Patterson for designing the book cover.

Who am I?

I am a witch...have been for a very long time, not the green-skinned warty kind obviously...the real sort, but I am also a working wife and mother who has also been lucky enough to write and have published a book or three. I love to learn, I love to study and have done so from books, online resources, schools and wonderful mentors over the years and still continue to learn each and every day, but have learnt the most from actually getting outside and doing it.

I like to laugh...and eat cake...

I am High Priestess of the Kitchen Witch Coven and an Elder at the online Wyld Witches/Kitchen Witch School.

I also have a regular Hedge Witch blog on Witches & Pagans and Beneath the Moon blog on Patheos Pagan.

My craft is a combination of old religion witchcraft, kitchen witchery, hedge witchery and folk magic. My heart is that of a kitchen witch. I am blessed with a wonderful husband, lovely children, a fabulous family and good friends.

Bibliography

Pagan Portals – Kitchen Witchcraft
Grimoire of a Kitchen Witch
Pagan Portals – Hoodoo Folk Magic
Pagan Portals – Moon Magic
A Kitchen Witch's World of Magical Plants & Herbs
A Kitchen Witch's World of Magical Foods
Pagan Portals – Meditation
The Art of Ritual
Arc of the Goddess (co-written with Tracey Roberts)
Pagan Portals – The Cailleach
Moon Books Gods & Goddesses Colouring Book (Patterson family)
Pagan Portals – Animal Magic

Websites
My website: www.rachelpatterson.co.uk
Facebook: www.facebook.com/rachelpattersonbooks
My personal blog: www.tansyfiredragon.blogspot.co.uk
Email: kitchenwitchhearth@yahoo.com
www.kitchenwitchhearth.net
www.kitchenwitchuk.blogspot.co.uk
www.facebook.com/kitchenwitchuk
www.thekitchenwitchcauldron.blogspot.co.uk

Be careful what you wish for with your wording and the thoughts you put out there,

be mindful of what you say and how you phrase it.

Let go of what you don't want and don't need to allow room for what you do...

Believe...

Chapter 1

The Journey

I would love to take you on a journey, one that leads us through the wilds of nature and back to the roots and bones of witchcraft, a natural witchcraft that works with the seasons and all the beautiful items that Mother Nature provides, drawing on magical folklore and a little bit of hedge witchcraft and gypsy magic too. No fancy schmancy tools or ceremonial rituals, this is about working with the source.

Mother Earth provides us with the changing of the seasons and within that turning of the year she gives us everything we need to work magic from natural energy in the form of storms, rain and sunshine to tangible items packed full of magical energy such as seeds, leaves and stones.

Just a walk through the fields, a forest or along the hedgerows or seashore will provide you with a whole host of natural magical items and will help you connect with the energy of the moment. Whatever season, month or day of the week it might be, nature is our own magical barometer.

You can tap into the energy from any place and each area or location will have its own unique energy. Forests, ponds, parks, streets, seashores and even city centres will all have that magical energy – it is just a case of plugging yourself into the source.

Select a tree or bush that is near you or your home. I have a silver birch tree at the end of my road and each day I look at it to see how it is and what stage it is at. In the winter it is dark and bare, then as spring approaches I see the tiny green buds starting to form, then they open and the green leaves start to show fully followed by catkins. Throughout the summer the leaves are bright green followed by a turning to yellow in the autumn before they float one by one down to the ground, ready once again for the winter slumber. It is my 'nature calendar', along with the plants in my own small garden. I can look out and tell exactly where we are in the cycle of the year.

Get to know your local area, take regular walks around your locality. Discover all the plants and trees that grow where you live. If you are close to a forest, a park or the sea you are very blessed. If you live in the city you may have to look a bit harder, but you will find Mother Nature there too. Have a look in local parks and recreation areas along with your local cemetery and churchyards. Take a notebook with you when you go out and write down what you see or take photos of the plants and trees so that you can identify them.

It doesn't matter whether you live in the city, in the country, on the side of a mountain or in a high-rise block of flats – magic is all around you.

You can throw away the structure and the rules (but only if you want to) and be wild! This is *your* journey, take the bits you like, the parts that work for you and throw them all into your very own and unique mixing pot to create a pathway that belongs to *you*.

Wheel of the Year

When I first started on my pagan journey I was presented with the Wheel of the Year, which it seemed most pagans worked with. I spent ages trying to remember the dates and learn the names and correspondences; even to this day I have to stop and think about it when trying to recall what is what! I also started dressing my altar for each sabbat and looking up all the correct colours, herbs and associations to know what to put on it. But I have to admit I started to lapse and I realised that I wasn't connecting with the celebrations and what I was doing was just a mechanical action because I thought I had to. As my journey has deepened and the years have passed I don't worry about any of it any more. I don't particularly work with the sabbats or at least not the set dates on the calendar. Especially as Mother Nature appears to be having a menopausal meltdown here in the UK at the moment and the seasons are all completely squiffy. I have summer bedding plants in the garden that have continued to flower all winter and daffodils and hawthorn flowering in January; it has all gone completely mad. In fact the winters in the past couple of years in the UK have not even been that cold. So it makes it quite difficult to celebrate the specific sabbats when nature isn't playing ball.

If you do follow the Wheel of the Year and it works for you then please, please continue to do so. I am not knocking the system, I just want to share with you how I work with the seasons and it is more on a monthly/weekly/stick-your-head-outside kind of basis rather than following the set dates on a calendar. It works for me, but it might not work for you.

I left the Wheel of the Year behind and started working with the energies of each month. It started a few years ago and has evolved to me working not just with the energies of each month, but sometimes even the specific energies of the week or the day. It is all governed by what nature and the weather are doing at any given time.

Also, the energies will vary depending on where you are in the world and how your seasons work. Our ancestors would have welcomed the first day of spring when they saw the signs of growth in the plants and the soil and the warming up of the weather, not because it was February 2nd (Imbolc). While it is useful to have the sabbat dates to use as a universal guide, the first signs of spring aren't always on a specific date. I struggled when spring was early or late and didn't arrive when the calendar told it to. With the UK having a very mild winter last year it was hard to acknowledge Yule/the winter solstice when the weather was so warm I didn't even need to wear a coat...

So now I follow my intuition and see what the energies of the day, week or month are going to bring. Be guided by nature, when she starts to send out the first shoots of spring on her plants, when the frosts have finished, when you open the door in the morning and you can feel the warmth of the early morning sun on your face. Listen to the birds, watch them building their nests, follow the progress of the baby birds learning to fly. Watch flowers opening on plants and leaves as they journey through the year from buds to green to orange and then fall. Nature is all around you, even if you live in the city there will be at least a tree or a bush that will give away the tell-tale signs of the seasons. Breathe in the air each day and see if you can tell when spring turns to summer and summer to autumn then on to the crisp cool air of winter; trust your senses.

It is a journey of discovery...

Journal

Yep I know...nearly every book out there says 'keep a journal' and you rush out, buy a beautiful notebook and new pens, write on the first day and then never look at it again (well if you are anything like me that's how it plays out). However...if you are going to be out and about and working with plants and natural items it might be an idea to keep a record of what you found, where you found it, what it looked like and so on, just for identification purposes or to know where to find it again. It can also be useful to note down the plant/seed/feather and what magical properties you found worked well for you when using that item.

I think it is also useful to keep a journal to record daily energies and weather patterns and, of course, a note of what magic you do, how the spell works and what the results are.

You don't need to hand write it, you can type it up on the computer. Just a suggestion...and I will give you a helping hand throughout this book with journal prompts, in case it helps. I won't be offended if you ignore them.

Energy and Ancestors

Each natural item you find or collect out in the wilds will have its own unique energy and that energy can be used for spell working or meditation. Each pebble will have an energy, probably very earthy, but if you find it by the ocean or a river then it will also have a watery element to it as well. Each tree, plant, flower, seed and twig will also carry its own special energy and will probably have a very definite character and personality. Tap into and connect with that energy, find out what the item is happy to offer you. Each one will have particular energies whether it is wisdom, knowledge, healing, protection...the list is long. No two twigs, no two pebbles, no two seed heads will be the same. It is a case of making that connection with the spirit of the item to find out. And you get used to people staring at you while you have a conversation with a twig...

Every space – whether it is your back garden, your living room, the city park or the middle of a field – has its own unique energy and history.

I live on the edge of a large city in a terraced house. My house was built in 1920, but before that there was another house on the land and before that and before that. I also live near the sea, the city being a port means it has attracted dwellings probably since man needed a roof over his head and somewhere nearby to catch food (the sea). The first recorded dwellings date back to the late 9th century and we have apparently had Romans, Normans, Saxons and all and sundry living here. So the land itself holds a huge amount of memories and echoes from our ancestors; oh, the tales it could tell!

It is important to connect with and get to know the energy and history of the ancestors of any space that you visit, especially if you want to work magic there or collect natural items. Obviously somewhere like a big city centre is going to be pretty sparse (but not completely devoid) of natural items, unless you want a cigarette butt or an old carrier bag, but the land beneath the concrete will have a special unique energy and it will be very happy to connect with a lovely caring soul after all the abuse it has probably suffered over the years. So, wherever you are, just take a moment to relax your mind and send out your spidey senses to connect with the land you are standing on.

If you are in a field or forest then the energy you connect with will be very different from that of the city centre, but it will be an experience wherever you are.

Whenever I have been to a group ritual I always connect with the land first and ask permission from the ancestors of that site to make sure they are okay with a load of pagans invading their area. I think it is a matter of courtesy, but also it is to ask them to lend their energies to the ritual as well. It pays to have the ancestors on your side...

I do the same if I am in a park, field, walking by a hedgerow, doing the school run or in the forest because I find it helps give me a sense of being – to connect with the land my feet are walking on. It can also give you a sense of what type of magical energies you can tap into and what energy it can lend to you.

If you get into the habit of connecting with your own house and garden it can also make you feel very comfortable and safe and help to keep your house and garden a happy and positive area to be in. Am I the only one who says 'hello' to my house when I come home?

Journal Prompt

Visit your local area and make a note of which places you visited, what time of the year and day it was and what energies you picked up on. Revisit those same places at different times of the year and keep a record of how or if the energy changes.

Go On, Get Connected...

I firmly believe that to be really connected to the earth and all the elements you need to be able to reach out and find the sparks and lines of energy that surround us, whether it is to discover what magical property a plant or tree can lend or to discover ancient ancestors and spirits of a part of the landscape.

To make that connection you will need to open your mind's eye – that psychic (for want of a better word) pathway. You don't need to be a skilled or trained psychic, but you do have to know how to open up and allow yourself to connect with outside energies; you also need to know how to protect yourself too.

Below are the basics to give you some guidelines to follow, but it may take practice before you master it all properly; please be careful.

There is energy in every living thing whether it is a flower, a crystal, a person or a building. You can draw upon energy from the elements such as the earth or the air around you and direct it for healing or spell work and you can also channel that energy through your body.

You can form and direct the energy and one of the most well used forms is the cone of power. This usually happens within a circle. The energy is raised by chanting and/or dancing in a circle, the energy builds and forms into an upwardly pointing cone that shapes itself in the centre of the circle and rises skywards. Once the cone is ready and it is felt that no more energy can be added it is released and sent to its destination.

On a smaller scale we raise and direct energy when we work a spell, for instance a candle spell. We would take the energy from the earth or the heavens, channel it through our body and out through our hands and into a candle; this will charge the candle with energy. We add our intent and any other ingredients, such as herbs and oils. Once the candle is burning it releases the energy we filled it with, that energy then goes on its merry way to fulfil the intent it was meant for. Or, in some cases, it goes towards a completely different intent because the universe likes to think it knows best...

You will need to open your mind and all your senses to see if you can detect the energy fields that are all around you.

Try it in a safe and familiar environment first, such as your home, especially if you have a willing human volunteer or even a pet. See if you can walk up to them from across the room with your eyes closed and feel their energy field with your outstretched hands. When you 'hit' a slight resistance you will have found the edge of their energy field.

Then try the same exercise with trees and plants; each one should have a completely different feel to the energy.

Once you have the hang of it, try it outside, although obviously not walking down the street with your eyes closed. Take yourself into your garden or into a field or forest, start by standing quietly just opening up your senses. What can you see? What can you hear? What can you smell? What can you sense? Allow your spidey senses to reach out and connect with the energy fields of the land, the trees and the plants.

Once you start opening yourself up to strange and unusual energy you will need to have some protection in place, particularly if you find yourself in the middle of a busy city centre. Having all your senses set to receptive while surrounded by hectic shoppers can be a very unpleasant experience.

You may also find if you are particularly sensitive that the spirit world will find you interesting too and there are some places, especially ancient ones, that have quite nasty histories or events that have echoes of energy. You don't want to pick those up.

Remember...*you* are always in control. If you find yourself being overwhelmed by spirit then just literally tell them to 'shove off' and not come back. If you are being bombarded with energy from too many things or people all at once, remember...*you* are in control. Bring up your psychic shield to keep them out.

Journal Prompt
Try some of the energy exercises suggested and make a note

of what you worked with and how the energy felt. Re-visit the exercises at a later date to try them again and see how different the energy felt.

Your Shield

Bringing in your psychic shield involves visualisation. Remember that energy field you felt around your willing volunteers? Well obviously you have an energy field too and you can strengthen that field for protection. For any Star Trek geeks out there I visualise the 'shields up, red alert' command in my mind and a protective bubble shield slides quickly into place around me.

You need the shield to protect you against negative energy, but you do still want the positive stuff to come through on a general basis. Visualise yourself in a flexible clear bubble with any negative energy pinging off the outside.

Another option is to visualise yourself pulling on a cloak of protection, wrapping it around you and pulling up the hood.

If you have really gotten yourself into a tight space you can, as a short-term measure, create a protective shield with a mirrored outside or a solid impenetrable wall. I would not recommend either of these for the long term though because, apart from being exhausting to maintain, they don't let any of the good stuff through and we all need positive energy.

Once you have the hang of shielding you can also fill the inside of your bubble with different colours of energy. For example, you might like to use yellow for happiness or pink for love. You can also visualise your bubble being filled with the elements, such as water to cleanse and purify.

It is your shield, tailor it to suit yourself.

Journal Prompt

Create your own shield, but try different options, various shapes, sizes, colours and styles. Try them out in a variety of situations and make a record of which ones worked best, how and why you think they did.

Getting Grounded

If you have been working a lot with energy or you have had a particularly spiritual ritual or experience you may find yourself feeling a bit lightheaded or even have a headache. This usually means you need to ground.

Energy work can make you feel very floaty and although it is a nice feeling for a while there will be a hard come-down afterwards. To avoid that you can ground yourself. This is a way of connecting with the energy of the earth and releasing any excess energy out from your system.

Some easy options are to clap your hands and stamp your feet, to eat something such as chocolate or cake (obviously my personal choice) or you can place your hands palms facing downwards onto the ground and allow the excess energy to drain back into Mother Earth.

If you are feeling really hyper you could work with a root grounding exercise:

Sit or stand comfortably and close your eyes.

Visualise roots beginning to grow from the soles of your feet or the base of your spine, as they grow twisting and turning they plunge down into the lush soil of Mother Earth.

The roots push down deeper into the soil allowing any excess energy to seep out and into the earth.

If you stretch down far enough your roots will tap into the centre of the earth and can draw up the balancing, comforting energy back into your body to bring you peace, calm and focus.

When you are ready, slowly draw your roots back up through the soil and into your body.

Open your eyes.

Journal Prompt

Try out different types of grounding exercises and see which ones work best. Keep a record of which ones you worked with and how effective they were.

The Sound of Silence or Noise

Sounds provoke all kinds of emotions and feelings, but they also inspire magic and can be used to raise energy.

There will always be particular sounds that you associate with a memory, person or place and these can be incredibly powerful.

I am lucky enough to live five minutes from the ocean so most mornings I am woken by the seagulls' dawn chorus, especially when they nest on the roof because their babies are noisy little beggars. But the sound of seagulls is one of my favourites, not just because it reminds me that I am very close to the sea, but also because it carries childhood memories of holidays spent at the beach.

New Year's Eve also brings a lovely sound (well lovely to me anyway); at the stroke of midnight all the ships and boats in the harbour sound their fog horns and it has become a bit of a tradition to wait and listen for them.

The sound of silence is also a precious one, albeit that we never really achieve complete silence because there will always be faint background noise, whether it is neighbours, the road outside or even quiet sounds of the leaves rustling in the breeze in the middle of a forest. I actually like to sit and meditate in silence sometimes and just allow my mind monkeys free reign... to pick up on the sound of next door's TV, people chatting as they walk past the house, birds in the garden or someone mowing their lawn – these are the sounds of life happening.

Apparently real silence that is completely devoid of sound is unbearable.

However, whether it is the sound of silence or your favourite noises, it can be used to create a meditative state, energy in a ritual or magic for spell working.

Drumming is the first noise that springs to mind. A couple of years ago I had the honour and pleasure of birthing my own stag skin drum and I absolutely love the sound of it, especially to meditate to or create energy in ritual. It also works very well to clear negative energy around the house. But you don't need an expensive drum, you can achieve the same kind of beat by hitting an old biscuit tin or even just clapping your hands. My favourite drum sound is that of big kettle drums, but I don't have the room at home to keep one...

Crystal or singing bowls seem quite popular for clearing negative energy or meditating to. Each one has its own unique sound, but I don't seem to have found one to suit me yet.

Singing, of course, works really well, especially if you are chanting to raise energy in circle or for a spell. Repetition is particularly effective and you don't need a good singing voice (which is a relief to me), just go with the flow. You don't even have to sing or chant a pagan song or rhyming words for your spell – follow your intuition. A good belted-out version of an ACDC track works just as well to raise energy.

It probably won't come as any surprise to you after my seagull confession that I love the sound of the ocean; it soothes and cleanses my soul. If you can't get to the seafront then there are plenty of YouTube videos and phone apps that can provide the sound of the ocean. The same goes for any sound from nature, such as the rain falling, forest background noise or birds singing.

You can raise energy in ritual using any sounds that work for you and also use the magic of noise to tie in with your spell work. Play a song that has a connection to your intent. For instance, for a prosperity spell you could play Money, Money, Money by Abba. For love spells you might pick any number of love songs, there are plenty out there.

Songs in themselves can bring up particular feelings and memories. If you are working magic or performing a ritual then use music/bands/singers that make you feel particularly witchy. I love the soundtrack from the film Practical Magic; it always makes me feel ready for magic. There are some amazing pagan bands and singers that write and perform tracks that can be used for specific sabbats and spell work.

The songs or sounds will be personal to you; if you like to have a soundtrack of rain playing when you work magic then go for it but if you prefer to play a bit of Bon Jovi to make your ritual magical then do that instead.

And if you prefer silence do that too...

Journal Prompt

Try out different sounds; listening to different styles of music, drumming, singing bowls, cymbals – whatever you want to work with – and keep a note of how each one made you feel.

Lost Your Connection?

One of the questions I get asked a lot is: 'I have lost my spiritual link or connection to my pathway, how do I get it back?'

Firstly...remember you aren't alone – it happens to us all, it really does.

Life likes to throw us challenges and slip blockages into our pathway – all of these and the usual mundane life stuff can get in the way of our spiritual journey.

If it has happened to you, don't panic.

Ask yourself some questions first:

- Is there a reason it has happened?
- Have I just been lazy or is it that real issues have cropped up?
- Has it happened because I need to tweak or change my pathway?
- Do I need some time away to sort things out?
- Have I been too busy?

All good questions and it might be one, two, all or none of these things, because we are individuals and everyone is different. But it can be sorted.

If I have found that life has taken me away from my spiritual journey for a reason then I deal with and sort out those reasons, knowing that when the time is right I will get back to my pathway; it will happen and there is no point worrying about things I cannot control. Sometimes the best course of action is to do nothing for a while…it can just slowly but surely creep back on its own.

If my practice has just slipped for whatever reason and I feel the call to get back into the swing then there are prompts and baby steps to help get back on track.

Usually the first thing I do is take down my altar, clean everything, sort it all out and re-dress with a nice fresh and bright altar space (it is good to clean your altar every so often anyway).

- Get back into the swing of things…but slowly.
- Start by meditating for a few minutes each day.
- Just spend a couple of minutes in front of your altar each day giving thanks for what you have.
- Read a book about your pathway; either a new one or re-read one that started your journey in the first place. Sometimes this happens because you are about to change your pathway into a new direction.
- Research a deity you have never worked with before.
- Listen to spiritual music.
- Sit and do some drumming or stand up and dance.
- Craft or create something such as an incense blend or a poppet.
- Get outside into your garden, the park, a forest or a trip to the seaside and re-connect with nature.
- Turn off your phone and your computer (step away from

Facebook) for a set amount of time each day. Start with 20 minutes and work your way up. Set that time aside to do something spiritual or to just sit and 'be'.

- Write a ritual, a chant, a spell or a spiritual poem.
- Set yourself some spiritual goals, don't be ambitious just set one goal a week or a month.
- Reach out to others – you are not alone in this experience. Seek out friends, family or other like-minded people face to face or via social media.
- Find a new area to study or research, something you haven't worked with before (tarot, crystals, astrology, whatever it might be).

Ultimately it happens to all of us at some point or other and often more than once. It can be uncomfortable and sometimes upsetting but...it can be resolved.

Don't panic and don't rush...your pathway is there waiting for you to step back onto...when you are ready.

Journal Prompt

If you are in the habit of keeping a regular journal you can note your feelings, emotions and general connection each day. It may help to look back over your journal to see if there is a pattern. Maybe you lose your connection when work is busy or family issues arise or it may be that the moon phases have some effect as well.

The Elements

Throughout this book you will find reference in one form or another to the four elements of earth, air, fire and water because essentially they are present in all of nature. I would encourage you to spend some time working with each element on an individual basis. Take at least a day to work with each one and totally immerse yourself in all aspects of that element. So for earth you might start with some gardening or a walk through the woods. Feel the earth not only beneath your feet but also throw your hands into the soil, feel the leaves and bark on the trees; touch, smell, see – use all your senses.

If you live near the sea or a river, then for water take a stroll along the water's edge. If the weather is good you might even like to take a swim. If you aren't near natural water then take a long bath or go to the local swimming pool and if it rains go and stand outside in it, get soaking wet and relish every moment of it.

Wait for a windy day to experience air. Find the highest hill or open space near you and stand in the middle with your arms thrown wide and let the wind whip itself around you.

For fire, if you have the space for a bonfire build one, or light up a fire pit or chimenea. Failing that, make a small fire in your cauldron.

Really connect with each element in its raw state, but also take a look at the mundane everyday chores that you do. Which element do you associate each one with? Cooking, reading, cleaning and laundry – what elements do they correspond with? You could even make a list of all the things you do in a day and work out what elements they connect with. Are you heavily weighted on working with one element? Do you need to add in some different element activities to bring balance?

Journal Prompt

Work with the element exercises and keep a record of what activities you did, where you went and how you felt with each element. You could even keep a daily record of what activities you do and which elements they correspond to and then look back to see what element balance or imbalances you have had.

Chapter 2

Altars and Offerings

Altars

An altar is a very personal thing and I firmly believe that unless you follow a strict tradition that sets the layout for you then you should 'go with the flow' with your altar and put things on it that your intuition guides you to.

An altar doesn't have to be big and it doesn't have to be fancy, just a vase of flowers on a windowsill is good enough to be a focal point for your altar.

One dictionary definition of an altar is: *'A table or flat-topped block used as the focus for a religious ritual, especially for making sacrifices or offerings to a deity.'*

That pretty much sums it up, although let's assume the 'sacrifices' bit is symbolic rather than young virgins left for the local dragon.

I also like to use my altar to pop spell workings on that are 'processing' and it gives me a focal point for meditation or prayers each day. But what you use your altar for is totally up to you.

A lot of altars will have traditional tools such as athames, wands and chalices with perhaps statues or representations of deity on as well, but for the 'into the wilds' witch anything goes and I do find mine is far more informal and definitely leans towards nature in a big way.

My main altar always has a vase of flowers, herbs or greenery from the garden along with pebbles and shells I have collected from the beach. Depending on the time of year it might have leaves, seeds and berries as well, usually placed around a central candle or offering dish.

I also believe an altar is fluid and can change weekly, monthly, sometimes daily depending on what you find or are gifted to put on it. Don't stick to any rules…it is your altar…work with it and see what you create. If it feels right put it there; if it doesn't then don't.

Traditionally an altar is in the north or east, but again go with what works for you. Sometimes you don't have the space to put it anywhere but in the west – seriously you won't be struck down by the gods.

If you are limited for space go with a windowsill or a shelf, the top of a bookcase, inside a cupboard or even a tray that you can keep hidden if needed and bring out when you want to work with it. If you have an outside space then you can even put an altar there; a large flat stone works well and you could even use a window box.

And if you don't want an altar…don't have one!

Offerings

When I collect anything from the wild I do like to leave an offering of some sort. If I am in the woods or fields I don't often have anything to hand so I give the plant or tree a blessing and a thank you. However, I do make offerings in my garden on a regular basis. It doesn't have to be anything fancy, in fact just feeding the birds or watering your plants is in a way an offering to Mother Nature. But, if you have collected natural items or been gifted something, it seems only good manners to say thank you with an offering. Maybe next time you are on a walk take a small bag of plant food and sprinkle some under a tree? I often make little salt dough offerings that I leave under trees when we hold a group ritual in the woods.

I also make specific offerings from a mixture of herbs and dried flowers, sometimes with a small crystal in as well, to sprinkle under trees or in hedgerows. These offerings can be made with a specific intent in mind – it might be for prosperity or healing. I leave them as a gift to the gods along with a prayer or request.

When I have finished holding a ritual I always pour some of the water or wine (or in the winter hot chocolate) onto the ground as a thank you along with crumbling up some of the cake we had in circle. (I know...throwing cake on the ground can be heart-breaking, but it is all for a good cause...)

Pouring a little milk and honey into a bowl and leaving it in your garden is also appreciated by the faerie folk.

Whatever you leave out in the woods, fields or hedgerows, please make sure it is biodegradable or a natural item. Plastic is a big no-no. And I know it is a beautiful experience to tie ribbons onto trees to make wishes or bring blessings, but manmade fibre ribbons don't degrade and the poor tree branches can get strangled as they grow.

Salt Dough Offerings

Salt dough is one of the easiest things in the world to make, and you can create just about anything from it. Use it with cookie cutters to make your own altar ornaments or make perfect offerings to leave in the garden or the woods.

Ingredients
4 cups (32oz) flour
1 cup (8oz) salt
1½ cups (12 fluid ounces) hot water
1 teaspoon vegetable oil

Combine the salt and flour, then add the water until the dough becomes elastic. Add the oil at this stage and knead the dough (if it is too sticky, add more flour). Once it is a good consistency, make your shapes with cookie cutters. Bake at 200C/400F/Gas 6 until hard (about 20-30 minutes). Leave the ornaments unpainted and unvarnished if you are going to use them as offerings.

Once they have cooled if you are making decorations you

can paint them with designs and symbols, and seal with clear varnish. If you are planning to hang them, poke a hole through the ornament *before* baking them. Then after you have varnished them run a ribbon or thread through the hole. You can also add a teaspoon of cinnamon and/or some glitter into the mixture before baking too.

Chapter 3

Energy of the Seasons and Days

Where you live in the word will influence what your seasons are and how they affect the energy around you. Here is a rough – and I mean rough – guide for working with the energy of the seasons in general. You have to take into account the weather, the area, the energy and all the other tiny elements that create the energy for any one particular day.

Spring

The element to work with for spring is air.

Spring is good to work magic for communication, travel, intellect, thought, mental powers, beginnings, freedom, teaching, divination, visualisation and study.

Summer

The element to work with for summer is fire.

Summer is good to work magic for action, passion, sexuality, anger, desire, energy work, power, strength, destruction, protection, banishing, purification and success.

Autumn

The element to work with for autumn is water.

Autumn is good to work magic for dreams, emotions, compassion, love, psychic healing, rest, cleansing, astral travel, death and rebirth and fertility.

Winter

The element to work with for winter is earth.

Winter is good to work magic for protection, grounding, the home, prosperity, fertility, ancestors, stability, wealth, strength, death and rebirth.

Obviously this is just a guide for magic that lends itself to the energy of the season, but don't restrict yourself, go with what works for you and what is needed or feels right at the time.

Energy of the Day

There are some time points during the day that lend themselves to magic. You don't have to work in tune with them, but I encourage you to give it a try and see what you get from it.

Dawn

When the sun rises over the horizon and a new day begins. As a working wife and mother I don't often have time to go and sit on the beach or on top of a hill to experience the sunrise, it just doesn't fit in with school runs and work schedules, but if you get a free morning it is worth making the effort even if you just watch it from your back garden.

This is a time of day when things move slowly. (Well for most of us that is true until after the first cup of coffee right?) Dawn does not have a sense of hurry about it, dawn likes to move gently. The sunrise lends itself to gentle magic that brings renewal, rebirth and restoration.

If you don't have the time or means to sit and watch the sunrise, how about greeting the sun when you get up in the morning? Whether the sun has been awake for a few minutes or a few hours it feels good to give it a nod of appreciation and a greeting to start your day.

Noon

The sun is now at the height of its travel and the clock strikes the daytime witching hour of twelve. It is an energy-filled time of the day, so make the most of it. Stand outside and shout to the world, the universe and the Divine let them know what your hopes, dreams and desires are...put it out there! It is a time of strength, passion and creativity.

The middle of the day has a really strong earth and fire energy to it, use that in your spell workings to the best advantage. If you don't have any workings to do then maybe get out your drum and join the sun in some energetic drumming and dancing.

Dusk

At the twilight of the day we are surrounded in a much calmer, somehow mysterious type of energy. It makes me think of the mists coming down onto the moors with shadowy magic about it.

This is a time of the day to look inwards for insight and inspiration, but also to connect with the Otherworld to gain clarity.

Take some time to look, listen and think; map out your web of life in front of you and follow the threads so that you know what adjustments need to be made.

Dusk is a very personal spiritual time of the day.

At the Midnight Hour

Midnight...the witching hour when all around us is in darkness. The midnight hour is perfect for spirit communication on a deep level to seek answers to the mysteries of life, the universe and everything.

Scrying, divination, meditation and candle magic work well in the dark hours and, of course, if the moon is not dark we can see and work with her beautiful face in full view.

Energy of the Days of the Week

Each day of the week also has its own specific energies and I would suggest you check first thing each morning to find out what the energy is for you. Take a step outside your house and breathe in, relax and allow your mind to connect with what the day has in store. See what words pop into your head or what feelings, emotions or insights the universe can throw your way. Taking just those few moments each morning will hopefully give you guidance for the rest of the day and point you in the right direction for what kind of magic will work best at that time.

If you want some kind of structure then the days of the week have particular magical intents that are specific and traditional to work with, but as always be guided by your own intuition. Here are some suggestions:

Monday: Fertility, intuition, emotions, clarity, wisdom, dreams, travel, feminine energy, peace, moon magic and illusions.

Tuesday: Success, strength, defence, protection, courage and challenges.

Wednesday: Communication, fortune, luck, changes, creativity, wild magic, cunning and the arts.

Thursday: Healing, strength, prosperity, wealth, abundance, protection and good health.

Friday: Romance, friendships, passion, fertility and love.

Saturday: Protection, wisdom, spirituality, cleansing and banishing.

Sunday: Prosperity, success, wealth, promotion, fame, personal achievements and acknowledgement.

Journal Prompt

Write down the energy that you feel each day, each week, each month and each season. Create your own personal list of energy correspondences.

Chapter 4

Ethical Wildcrafting

Before we go any further I would like to just mention here... for any objects, whether they are seeds, buds, sticks or feathers, try to use items that have been gifted rather than, for example, plucking feathers from a live bird (which would probably be difficult and dangerous anyway). Use sticks and leaves that have fallen to the ground rather than cutting them from the tree or plant.

Ethical wildcrafting is the practice of harvesting plants and trees conscientiously, to avoid damaging the health of the plant population or the overall ecological system. With seeds and fruits maybe just make sure you ask the plant first if it is okay for you to harvest the fruits and leave an offering in place. Please don't take more than you need, leave enough for others, for animals and birds and, in the case of seeds, for the plant to re-seed itself. Make sure to only take a small amount and leave enough of the plant in situ so that it can continue to grow. Please also note that some plants in the wild are protected and even on the verge of extinction.

Every plant, seed, flower, herb, tree, pebble, stone, sea shell – in fact all 'living' and natural items – have an energy to them. Some see it as an individual energy for each item, a character or a personality if you like. Some see it as a spirit that resides within the natural item. However you see it, this energy is specific to each item so each plant will have its own unique energy and every single shell on the beach will have its own special energy too. We can tap into that energy and connect with the spirit of the natural item to gain insight, wisdom and even healing. Just remember to ask first because some of them can be shy or grumpy...some may not want to work with you at all. In those situations just thank the plant/tree and leave it be. Mother Nature wants to help you and is happy to share whatever energy you need, just remember to be polite.

How to Harvest

If you are picking flowers or plants for magical workings then below is a basic guide.

If you can collect fallen flowers, seeds, twigs and so on, then even better, because the plant has already finished with them, but if you want to remove them directly from the plant, always be careful not to damage the plant itself. Only take what you need, leave enough of the plant to continue growing and always ask permission from the plant first.

Use a sharp knife or cutters because blunt blades leave jagged edges, which can leave the plant open to infection.

Flowers

It is usually best to pick flowers when the bud is fully open and cut the stalk at the first leaf joint. If possible pick them in the morning before the sun gets too hot. To dry lay them out on a kitchen towel in a warm dry place (I put them on trays in the conservatory). Once dried store them in a dark glass jar with a detailed label (what they are and the date you harvested them). The dark glass prevents fading from sunlight.

Seeds

Seed harvesting should be done on a dry day. You don't want to take home seed heads that are all soggy from the rain because they will go mouldy. Once seed pods have changed from green to brown and can be easily split, you can begin collecting flower seeds. Cut the pod or seed head from the stalk and pop it into a paper bag. Or you can hang seed heads on stalks upside down with a paper bag tied around to catch the seeds.

Bark

You can successfully harvest small amounts of bark direct from the tree; birch trees in particular lend themselves to this practice without suffering too much, but...and here's the thing...I can never bring myself to strip bark direct from a tree. I do, however, pick up pieces of fallen bark or strip bark from branches that have been removed by forest wardens or that perhaps a storm has knocked down. If you don't harvest bark properly, you can kill the tree. If you want to give it a try it is best to only do so in the autumn when the tree is starting to prepare for winter and is drawing all its energy into the core. Depending on how much bark you need you can just shave a little piece direct from the tree or cut a small branch off and use all the bark from that. But do your research first, identify the type of tree as there are different methods for different trees – Google should be able to help you with the finer details.

Roots

To harvest roots from a plant first of all check that it is healthy looking and that you have identified it correctly. Some people find the largest plant or what they call 'the grandmother plant' and ask permission to harvest some roots, if the answer comes back as a yes then you can harvest one or two of the smaller plants that surround the grandmother. Roots are best gathered in spring or early autumn. Although I personally think autumn is best because the plant has been allowed to grow, flower and spread seed over the summer.

Dig the plant out carefully and, if possible, just trim pieces of the root from the ends and then pop the plant back into the ground. If this isn't possible then please make sure there are plenty of others from the species growing in the surrounding areas. Once you get them home, wash off as much soil as you can then dry them well. To dry roots I find that chopping them into smaller pieces works best then I lay them out on a flat tray and put them in a dry, dark place. When they are completely dried they will feel dry to the touch but still be slightly spongy. Store them in dark glass jars with detailed labels.

Leaves

If you are harvesting herbs then it is best to pick them in the morning and either tie them into bundles and hang them up or lay them out separately on trays in a dry, dark place (leaving them in sunshine fades the colour). For plant leaves such as trees or wild plants you can look in the autumn for fallen leaves, which will already be dry, or you can pick them directly from the plant or tree. Be careful not to tear or rip them from the plant, just gently pluck each one. Then lay them out to dry. For a lot of the fresh green plant leaves, they usually keep their colour and dry better if you harvest them direct from the plant or tree in the spring. Again store them in dark glass jars as sunlight can fade them.

Berries

Now these are a bit trickier to dry. With something like a blackberry you are probably better picking them ripe and eating them straight away or they freeze well. If you want to use blackberry in magical workings then go for the petals of the flower or the leaves. Leave the fruit for yummy puddings. However, berries from the hawthorn, for instance, are much easier to dry. Pick them ripe and thread them onto a string using a needle, then hang them up to dry.

In the Hedgerow

We associate hedgerows with long winding country lanes, but actually a lot of cities and towns have hedgerows. There might be one near you even if it is just the one outside the front of your garden or alongside the local school. It doesn't matter if it is a hedge stuffed with nesting birds and packed full of berries or a sad neglected hedge littered with old crisp packets, it is still a hedge and still full of magic, you just need to know how to tap into it and use the magic it can provide for you.

When you are walking through the local countryside with the hedgerows on either side or when you are walking back from the school run past a few hedges at the front of houses what do you feel? Next time you are there send out your spidey senses and see if you can connect with the energies of the hedge...what type of plant is it? How does it feel? What magic can it help you with? What can you do for it? If you are in the middle of a busy high street you might want to try to look a little less suspicious so rather than standing there talking to it maybe just put your hand out to connect with the leaves or branches and close your eyes...allow the link to be made.

Chapter 5

Fields and Fens

Field, meadow, pasture and fen...lots of different names, but what do they mean?

A meadow is generally a small patch of agricultural grassland often spattered with wild flowers, but not intensively managed. They are often poor soil and not easily accessible by farm machinery. A meadow usually has a boundary made from old stone walls, woodland or hedges.

A field, however, is very similar to a meadow, but will be managed more intensively and often filled with a particular crop.

A pasture is land that is used to keep cattle on for grazing.

Then we have a prairie, which is a term used in North America for a large open area of grassland.

And a fen...which is basically soggy. It is a low and marshy piece of wetland that frequently floods. Think grassy marsh, swamps and peat bogs.

I have to be honest and say that I would rather be stood in the middle of a meadow with the grasses swaying and the bees buzzing around the wildflowers than in the middle of a forest, but each person will have their own favourite place to be.

The key point with any meadow, field or flat open area is just that...it is open. You will get the amazing feeling of freedom and space standing in the middle. You may also find a huge amount of different types of grasses growing and grass makes excellent magic especially for something like knot spells.

Grass Magical Properties: Protection, psychic powers, knot magic, abundance and binding.

Element: Earth.

Journal Prompt

Research your local area and find out what fields and fens you can visit easily (and with permission). Make notes about what plants you find there, the time of year, what the weather was like and what energies you felt. Revisit at different times and note the changes.

Field Meditation

Make yourself comfortable.

Relax and allow the worries and stresses of the day to fall away. Close your eyes and focus on your breathing, deep breaths in…deep breaths out, then visualise the following:

As your world around you dissipates you find yourself in the middle of a field, the sun is shining and the sky is a clear bright blue.

You are surrounded by tall grass that reaches up to your waist and it is scattered with beautiful wild flowers of all colours.

You can hear the bees busily buzzing around, zipping from flower to flower, and the sounds of the birds in the trees at the edge of the field happily singing to each other.

There is a very slight breeze that dances across your skin and carries the scent of the flowers with it.

Just ahead you notice that the grass has been flattened so you make your way to it. On the ground in the space is a blanket and some beautifully patterned cushions, so you lie down and make yourself comfortable.

From your position you are now looking up at the bobbing heads of grass and flowers swaying gently in the summer breeze.

Breathe in the scents and listen carefully to the sounds from all around you.

What messages are there for you? Listen very carefully…the whispering may come from the grasses or the wild flowers, the messages may come from the bees as they buzz past you or the connection may come from the earth that you are lying on.

Spend some time listening and learning...

When you are ready give thanks for the wisdom and clarity that has been shared with you.

Stand up and take a final look around the field and know that you can always return if you want to.

Slowly open your eyes and come back to this reality, wriggling your fingers and toes.

Journal Prompt

Work with the meditation and write down any thoughts, images or messages that come to you.

Knot Magic

Long stems of grass really lend themselves to knot magic, but you can also use thin stems of plants such as ivy or even twine, string or ribbon.

If you have the patience you can 'weave' a ball of grass and hang it up in your home to provide protection; you can also plait the longer stems to make witch ladders.

Long stems of grass can also be used for bindings and to control a person's movements, to stop them from causing harm or to tie something down, magically of course, not literally...

You can bind pretty much any intent by sealing it with a knot. If you want a new job, a new dress or maybe a holiday, pick your intent and tie the energy into a knot.

And of course, that love kinda thing works very well with knot magic. Whether you want to tie your current relationship together or whether you want to just bring love your way, this can be done by binding the intent into a knot. Think about the handfasting or even some church weddings where the couple's hands are tied together... I must put a disclaimer in here, with love magic I find it personally wise to be mindful of the 'free will of another' thing. It is obviously your choice if you choose to bind someone to you, but I urge you to think very carefully about the consequences.

Tie a knot with the intent of prosperity, good health and luck and hang it over your front door so that every time someone walks in they bring the positive energy with them.

If you are crafty you can of course take the knot magic a step further and crochet, weave or knit energy into something beautiful by putting the magic in as you create.

Need to boost your memory or remember something important? Tie a knot in a piece of string and seal it in. When you see the knot you will know that you have to remember something...of course then you have to remember exactly what is it that you needed to remember...

Then there is the flip side of binding and knot magic in that you can undo it too. You can unbind a spell, a curse, an influence or negative energy. You do this simply by binding the intent into the knot and then unravelling it.

Curses and hexes can be bound into knot magic – just say your curse out loud as you tie each knot.

You can keep the knot magic simple by literally just visualising or saying the intent as you tie the knot or you can put on a whole ritual with candles, incense and plinky plonky music, the choice is yours. You can even sprinkle the knot with corresponding herbs or dab it with anointing oil.

Journal Prompt

Keep a note of any knot magic that you work, what you did, what you used and how the result turned out.

Chapter 6

Forests and Woodlands

What is the difference between a forest and a woodland? In this case it seems that size really does matter...

A forest is large with the trees packed in so tightly that barely any sunlight makes its way through the canopy of leaves. Forests can have deciduous or evergreen trees or a mixture of both, but they cover a large area and are full of lots of different types of wildlife. They will also have shrubs, undergrowth and grasses. Forests also usually have a higher canopy cover than a woodland area.

A wood is a dense formation of trees, but is much smaller than a forest, although it is larger than a grove. (Have I lost you yet?) You will find a lot more sunlight makes its way through the upper canopy of trees in a woodland area than it does in a forest.

Did you know that there are also different types of forest? This depends on the location in the world. Boreal forests are found near the poles, tropical forests around the equator and the mid-latitude area has temperate forests.

Whether it is a woodland or a forest, it is a mini ecosystem that is vital to us as humans. As the trees and plants convert carbon dioxide into breathable air they also help regulate the climate, purify water and even provide protection against strong winds and floods.

A grove is a small group of trees with minimal or no undergrowth, which can be made up from any type of tree but often fruit trees.

And then we have a coppice, which is usually a small managed group of trees often used for cutting.

And here are some more:

Brake: A small group of shrubs, briars or fallen trees.

Coombe: The head of a wood in a valley.

Copse: A very small wood.

Covert: A dense group of shrubs or trees sometimes used for game.

Dingle: A deep wooded valley or dell.

Spinney: A copse that homes game.

Stand: A small group of trees.

Thicket: Shrubs and briars growing together.

Forests, woodlands or whatever you call them are magical places full of potential and possibilities with any amount of hidden surprises...if you have one near you I encourage you to investigate not just once or twice, but try to visit at different times of the year because each season will bring out more magic. Not only that, but trees are usually happy to provide us with all sorts of magical goodies such as leaves, twigs and seeds, all of which have magical uses. Forests, or woodland or whatever group of trees you are in can also provide feathers and small bones as well.

Journal Prompt

Research your local area and find out what forests or woodlands you can visit easily and with permission. Make notes about what plants you find there, what time of the year, what the weather is like and what energies you feel. Revisit at different times and note the changes.

Grove Meditation

Make yourself comfortable.

Allow the stresses and the worries of the day to slip away. Close your eyes and focus on your breathing, deep breaths in... and deep breaths out.

As your world around you dissipates you find yourself in the centre of a grove of trees. The grass beneath your feet is short and stubby and you are surrounded by a small circle of tall trees.

The sky is beginning to get dark as the sun is setting on the horizon, but there is still enough light to see clearly by and you realise that it is because there are lanterns hung in the branches of the trees around you.

The air is warm and you feel comfortable and safe.

You make your way towards the edge of the circle of trees and as you get closer you realise they are fruit trees heavily laden with apples.

You reach up and pluck one of the ripe apples from the tree and take a bite. It is fresh, juicy and sharp and the juice runs down your chin.

Deciding to sit down beneath the apple tree you make yourself comfortable within the roots and lean with your back against the trunk.

As you eat the apple you hear a voice speaking to you...

The tree is talking to you, so you respond. It asks your name and if you have any questions, so you ask away...

Once you have finished your conversation you give thanks for the wisdom you have gained and bury your apple core in the soil under the tree.

Take one last look around the grove of trees then, when you are ready, come back to reality.

Slowly open your eyes and wriggle your fingers and toes.

Journal Prompt

Work with the meditation and write down any thoughts, feelings or messages that came to you.

Trees

This is such a huge subject it has books all to itself, but I will cover just a little about our lovely trees.

I am lucky enough to have woodland a five-minute drive away and forest a ten-minute drive away from me, but I don't always have access to a car, so some days I have to make do with the trees that line the street on the walk to school with my youngest or the tree (that was supposed to be a bush but is now 15 feet tall) that grows in my garden.

We need trees...the planet needs trees and not just because they look amazing, but also because they take in carbon dioxide and release oxygen, oxygen being the stuff that we as humans need to breathe – definitely important.

Trees have their roots deep in the earth, which is their connection to the Underworld/Otherworld; their trunks are in the land of men or the Middle World; and the top branches reaching up to the sky connect to the Upper World. In fact a tree is an excellent focus point for journeying or as I do, hedge riding. The tree is an access point to the three different realms.

There is a huge joke about 'tree huggers', but seriously hugging a tree does you the world of good and it can also lend you energy, healing, knowledge and wisdom. However...don't forget to ask the tree's permission first, not all trees want to be hugged and not all trees will be happy to work with you. Ask first and respect the answer you are given.

Trees are also our seasonal compass. Bear in mind that I don't live in a little cottage in the middle of a forest, seriously not all witches do...shocking I know. I live on the edge of a large city, but we do have the odd tree dotted around to use as a guide.

Have a delve into history and read about all the different trees that appear in myths and legends because there are a huge amount of stories ranging across different cultures and pantheons.

Journal Prompt

Research your area and find out what varieties of trees you have.

I bet you will be surprised how many there are. Also have a look and see what types of tree are native in your location as well.

Tree Magic

Each variety of tree has specific magical properties and you will find on closer inspection that each individual tree has its own unique personality. To discover what each tree means and what magical properties it has and is happy to share with you I suggest meeting each tree and asking. However, I have listed below a general guide for tree magic. You can use seeds, bark, twigs and leaves from a specific tree to bring the magical property they hold into your magical workings. Or you can just print off a picture of the tree to use as the basis of spell work. And, of course, if the tree is happy to gift you a large enough twig you can make a wand with it.

Alder: Confidence, bravery, spiritual growth, spiritual protection and journeys.

Apple: Fertility, love, peace, joy and faerie magic.

Ash: Communication, mental abilities, wisdom, understanding, spiritual love, balance, protection and weather magic.

Beech: Divination, healing, wisdom, ancestors and desires.

Birch: Cleansing, rebirth, renewal, emotions, psychic protection, moon magic and new beginnings.

Cedar: Cleansing, protection and spirit work.

Cherry: Grounding, centring, stability, focus, intuition, divination, spirit work, healing, love and animal magic.

Elder: Banishing, protection, changes, healing and faerie magic.

Elm: Fertility, death and rebirth, goddess, grounding, focus and faerie magic.

Hawthorn: Psychic protection, creativity, confidence, purification, patience, insight, weather magic, Otherworld, banishing and faerie magic.

Hazel: Knowledge, creativity, love, change, wisdom, inspiration and magic of all kinds.

Holly: Strength, power, protection, purity, beauty and prosperity.

Ivy: Strength, spiritual growth, protection, determination and success.

Maple: Spiritual healing, travelling, knowledge, communication and abundance.

Oak: Truth, knowledge, protection, long life, healing, centring, grounding, focus, intuition, courage, prosperity and leadership.

Pine: Centring, focus, dragon magic, protection, truth, abundance, purification, fertility and healing.

Poplar: Divination, banishing, hope, rebirth – a general multi-purpose wood.

Vine: Faerie magic, happiness, rebirth, knowledge and spirituality.

Walnut: Astral travel, weather magic and motivation.

Willow: Death and rebirth, emotions, healing, love, divination and psychic work.

If you want to work with a tree on a one-to-one basis– i.e. the tree is physically right in front of you – approach slowly and see if you can send your thoughts out to the tree; ask if you have permission to come closer. Hopefully you will get a good positive feeling or even the whisper of acknowledgement in your head. If the energy feels hinky in any way then just thank the tree and move on to another one.

Once you feel you have had permission, slowly walk up to the tree and touch the bark with the palms of your hands. This helps you make a direct connection to the tree and the dryad/spirit within. If you have questions, need healing or just want to spend time with the tree then the best way is to sit beneath it with your back leaning against the trunk. Spend some time, talk, ask questions and most importantly listen. Trees are ancient and they carry a huge amount of knowledge and wisdom. Once you are finished remember to thank the tree and if possible leave an offering; just a splash of water is fine, but anything natural will work such as pebbles, shells and flowers.

Journal Prompt

Research your local area and find out what trees grow in your locality. Make notes about each one with pictures or sketches of the leaves, flowers and seeds to help identify them. Revisit at different times of the year to see and record the changes.

Tree Meditation

Make yourself comfortable.

Allow the stresses and worries of the day to slip away. Close your eyes and focus on your breathing, deep breaths in...and deep breaths out.

As your world around you dissipates you find yourself standing on a grassy pathway that stretches out in front of you for what seems like forever. Lining each side of the path are rows and rows of trees of all different shapes, colours and sizes.

The sky is bright blue dotted with a few wispy white clouds. The weather is warm, but has an autumnal feel about it.

You start to walk along the grassy footpath, stopping and looking at each tree. There are so many and all different. You recognise some of them; an oak, a birch, an apple, a beech tree, but some are less familiar and seem to be from faraway places.

As you walk one of the trees draws you to it...what tree is it?

You reach out your hand and touch the trunk and make an instant connection. You can feel the spirit of the tree, the sap running through it and the life it holds within.

You have made a direct link with this tree for a reason; what energy and insight does it have to share with you? Do you need to ask any questions?

Spend some time...

When you are ready thank the tree for sharing its energy and wisdom with you.

If you then want to seek out another tree you can carry on walking...

If you are finished for now know that you can always come back to this space.

When you are ready come back to this reality, slowly open your eyes and wriggle your fingers and toes.

Journal Prompt

Work with the meditation and make a note of what images, thoughts or messages came to you.

Ogham

One of the most well known tree divination systems is the ogham; symbols of a tree language that it has been suggested dates back to the 4th century. Sometimes called the Celtic Tree Alphabet, each stroke of the ogham corresponds to a letter of the alphabet.

The ogham originally contained 20 letters, but later five more were added, making five groups of five characters. Ogham inscriptions have been found throughout the United Kingdom. It uses the names of trees to associate with individual characters. Most of the inscriptions found are made up of personal names and marks that claim ownership of the land.

The Ogham Meanings

Birch: Beginning, renewal, youth, change and good fortune.

Rowan: Protection, expression, connection, strength and healing.

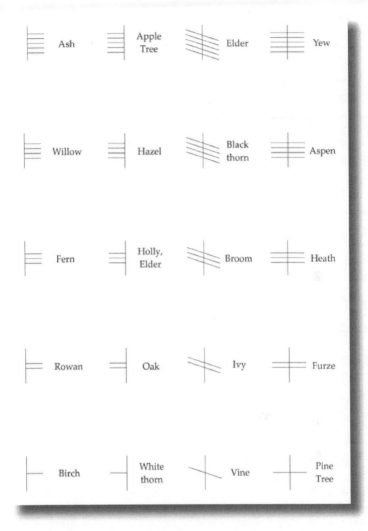

Alder: Endurance, strength, passion, divination, intuition and the arts.

Willow: Imagination, intuition, vision, fertility and psychic abilities.

Ash: Connection, wisdom, surrender, spiritual inspiration and action.

Hawthorn: Contradiction, consequence, relationships, protection and purification.

Oak: Strength, stability, nobility, new pathways, protection and leadership.

Holly: Action, assertion, objectivity, balance, justice, courage and growth.

Hazel: Creativity, purity, honesty, intuition, divination and perception.

Apple: Beauty, love, generosity, choices and healing.

Vine: Introspection, relaxation, depth and psychic abilities.

Ivy: Determination, change, patience, exploration and transformation.

Reed: Harmony, health, growth, fertility, protection and love.

Blackthorn: Discipline, control, perspective, fate and rebirth.

Elder: Transition, evolution, continuation, change and renewal, career and health.

Fir: Clarity, achievement, energy, foresight, grounding and new projects.

Gorse: Transmutation, resourcefulness, exposure and prosperity.

Heather: Dreams, romance, feelings, spirit, healing, success and fertility.

Poplar/Aspen: Victory, transformation, vision, inner guidance and rebirth.

Yew: Transference, passage, illusion, death and rebirth and new beginnings.

Yep I know technically some of the above aren't trees, but they are in the ogham!

Ogham sets can be easily made by painting the symbols onto twigs, pebbles or lolly sticks and then used for divination as you would a set of runes. However, I like to use the symbols for spell work; carving them into candles or writing on petition slips.

Celtic Tree Calendar

The date and use of the Celtic tree calendar is up for debate.

Robert Graves in his book *The White Goddess* (pub. 1948) suggested that the Celts used a lunar calendar that had 13 months, each with 28 days and each of those months was associated with a specific tree. Graves having taken the idea from antiquarian Edward Davies who made the first suggestion of it in the early 19th Century. I will leave it up to you as to whether you believe the Celts used this system or not...

Birch: 24th Dec-Jan 21st
Rowan: 22nd Jan-18th Feb
Ash: 18th Feb-17th March
Alder: 18th Mar-14th Apr
Willow: 15th Apr-12th May
Hawthorn: 13th May-9th June
Oak: 10th June-7th July
Holly: 8th July-4th Aug
Hazel: 5th Aug-1st Sept
Vine: 2nd Sept-29th Sept
Ivy: 30th Sept-27th Oct
Reed: 24th Nov-28th Oct
Elder: 25th Nov-23rd Dec

Each tree month carries the magical properties of the tree that it is associated with so you could use that as the basis for your magical spell workings.

Your Own Tree Calendar

You could also create your own tree calendar and even your own tree divination system. Pick tree species that are local to your own area or expand across the globe then write out a list of months and associate a tree with each one. Or write down the names of a set of trees and create your own divination meanings for each one.

Journal Prompt

Make a journal just for the trees in your area and fill it with photographs, sketches and drawings of the leaves, the bark, the seeds and flowers so you can easily identify the tree each set is from. This will give you a record of what they look like in each season.

Chapter 7

Nature Spirits and Faeries

Dryads/Tree Spirits

Anyone who works with the animism belief (as I do) will discover tree spirits.

Animism is defined as: *'The attribution of a living soul to plants, inanimate objects, and natural phenomena.'* The word animism is derived from the Latin word 'anima', which means 'breath' or 'soul'. It is the belief that a soul or spirit exists in every object, whether it is an animal, plant or rock.

The belief that spirits (or ghosts as they were sometimes believed to be) lived in trees goes back a long way, the Old Testament has references to sacred groves.

Celts, Romans and Egyptians, among other cultures, all believed in tree spirits. In fact in India the banyan tree is especially sacred and shrines are built under the trees to honour the spirit that dwells within.

If you look up one dictionary definition of the word 'dryad' it says: *'In folklore and Greek mythology – a nymph inhabiting a tree or wood,'* which is just about spot on. Each tree will have its own inner spirit as all plants do, but tree spirits are specifically named dryads.

Greek mythology tells us of dryads, hamadryades and oreads – female nature spirits that dwell within trees, woodlands, groves and forests, with a particular fondness for oak trees. All of the texts and images from mythology seem to depict dryads as female.

A hamadryade is born with the tree and bound to it for the entire lifespan of the tree; when the tree dies so does the hamadryade.

Dryads can be found within their own tree or very close by

49

as they never venture far from it. They are incredibly shy and if startled will quickly disappear into the tree.

There are different types of dryads:

Meliae: Live specifically in ash trees.

Oreads: Nymphs of mountain conifers.

Hamadryades: Usually found in oak and poplar trees, especially those that are in sacred groves or beside a river.

Meliades or Epimelides: Apple and fruit tree dwelling dryads.

Daphnaie: Laurel tree dryads.

Nymphai Aigeiroi: Black poplars.

Ampeloi: Grape vines.

Karyai: Hazel nut trees.

Kranelal: Cherry trees.

Pteleai: Elm trees.

Orelades is the general name given to nymphs of the mountains, Alseides of the sacred groves, Napalal of the valleys and Aulonides of the glens.

In Celtic mythology you will find the same spirits, but with different names such as tree nymphs, sidhe draoi or faerie druids. The world of Faerie is vast and there are many, many different types of fae associated with trees and woodlands.

Lesidhe are known as woodland guardians. These are the wood spirits that cause a bit of chaos and trouble within the woods for humans by scaring and confusing them.

Tree spirits (also known as poldies, pottons or skeagh-shee) choose to live among the trees and are sometimes confused with elves. Some like to live near a particular tree others may wander nomadically between species.

Blackthorn sprites (or lunatishee) are guardians of the blackthorn; they are complete anti-social hermits who prefer to come out only at night to bathe in the moonlight.

Oak men (also known as inifri duir, bodachan na croibhe moiré) are what it says on the tin...they live in ancient oak trees.

Elder mothers (elder witches, burtree witches) the spirit of the elder tree (obviously). Folklore beliefs were such that witches were thought to transform themselves into elder trees and others believed that elder trees housed the souls of dead witches.

Mythology and folklore have a huge amount of stories and details for dryads and tree spirits. If you are interested it is a fascinating subject to do some research on.

For the purpose of finding your local dryads you will need to seek out the trees in your neighbourhood and connect with them.

Devas/Plant Spirits

Of course, if each tree has its very own spirit then it follows that every plant does too. And of course each one is unique and has an individual character and personality.

Plant spirits can be called upon to help with knowledge and guidance, but particularly with healing. A spiritual journey can be undertaken to meet with a plant spirit to obtain healing. Each plant will offer a different and unique type of healing.

The word 'deva' may have originated in Persia and migrated to Greece and then on to the rest of Europe. The word 'deva' is Sanskrit and means 'shining one' and this may refer to the aura that is said to shine around the plant as it is worked with. A deva is a plant guardian, but it also has other tasks such as healing plants, helping them grow and protecting and nurturing a whole area of plant life – basically they are nature's architects.

Tree/Plant Spirit Meditation

Make yourself comfortable.

Allow the stresses and worries of the day to slip away. Close your eyes and focus on your breathing, deep breaths in...deep breaths out.

As your world around you dissipates you find yourself standing beside an old red brick wall that stretches out in front of you as far as you can see. You start to walk along and spot an ancient wooden door set into part of the wall ahead so you make your way towards it.

Standing in front of the big wooden door with large rusty hinges you put your hand out and push...the door resists a little, but then with a loud creak it swings slowly open.

As the door opens it reveals a delightful scenic garden beyond... you step through the gateway.

The garden is in full bloom and packed with flower beds of all varieties, vegetables in neat uniform rows, herbs in big pots and around the edge of the walls are fruit trees of all kinds interspersed with climbing roses and trailing clematis. It is breathtaking...

The scents that are being carried around on the gentle breeze are intoxicating and the sound and sight of the bees and butterflies flitting around is amazing.

As you wander around taking it all in and investigating each section you notice that right in the centre of the garden is a wooden bench so you head towards it.

You make yourself comfortable on the bench and then find your intuition is prompting you to ask whether there is a tree or plant spirit that would like to connect with you...you ask out loud...

You may get an answer straight away or it may take a few moments, but you hear a sound and are directed to a particular area of the garden. Make your way to the plant or tree that you are drawn to.

Reach out and smell the flower, touch the leaves or connect with the bark of the plant or tree; be guided by your intuition. Make the link and ask what information, guidance or energy the plant or tree has for you.

Ask questions and listen...

Spend as much time as you need connected to the plant or tree spirit.

When you are ready, thank the spirit and break the link.

You might like to find a watering can in the garden and water the plant or tree as a gesture of thanks too.

Make your way back through the garden and out of the garden gate in the wall.

Know that you can always return to this garden when you want to.

Slowly and gently come back to this reality. Open your eyes and wriggle your fingers and toes.

Journal Prompt

Work with the meditation and make a note of what images, thoughts or spirits came to you and any messages they gave to you.

The World of Faerie

Dryads, tree and plant spirits and devas are all technically part of the world that we refer to as Faerie, which covers everything from tiny flower spirits right up to ogres and a huge assortment of beings in between.

I have covered only a couple of faerie groups because it is such an enormous area. You may well encounter all sorts of faeries when out in the wilds.

I think the general idea is to think of faeries as little flittery things with gossamer wings, stripy tights and a skirt made from flowers. There are of course many, many races and species of faerie – as wide and diverse as ours, if not more so, and quite possibly none of them have ever worn stripy tights. Don't be fooled by the 'sparkly, glittery fluff' idea of their image...

The Faerie realm is just that, a realm in its own right that runs alongside ours and every so often our worlds intersect. Media and literature would have us imagine all sorts of wonderful, mystical, faraway places to be the land of the fae. But in actual fact Faerie is all around us. Nature provides us with the portals, we just need to open our inner eyes to see them.

The Fae do like meeting with humans, but they are quite particular. The most important thing to remember is that the Fae demand respect.

We would never ever contemplate destroying nature – because of who we are and what we believe, but what we also need to think about is that nature is where the fae hang out. To destroy their habitat or meeting places would not put you in their good books.

The Fae are famous for their sense of humour and practical jokes, so you also need to be able to laugh with them. The folk of Faerie do not play by the same rules that we do; their sense of justice, judgement and morals can be completely different to ours. The world of Faerie has dark and light just as our world does.

If you are open with them, respect them and their habitat, honour them and show them your trust then you will be able to work with them. Most importantly *never command them or demand anything from them*, this sort of action with break all ties with them. If you would like to work with them then invite them or request their company as you would with a special friend.

And, although it might seem bizarre, never say 'thank you' to a faerie, they don't like it. Whatever the reason is (I am not sure) perhaps it is just something 'too human' or maybe they don't like the tone of it. Instead of thanking them, leave them a gift.

I would suggest you always work with protection when working with the Fae. Laziness and complacency when working with faeries can lead to undesirable results. Perform protection and grounding routines every time.

And, of course, *never* dance or partake of food and drink when on a visit to the realm of the Fae. This can lead to entrapment. Although I have heard that witches are said to be among the only mortals who may blur these rules slightly, personally I wouldn't chance it...

Chapter 8

Leaves, Sticks and Seeds

Leaves

Mother Nature provides a dizzying array of leaf colours and shapes, which change throughout the year in some cases.

I only pick leaves from plants if they are herbs or the plant is in my garden and needs trimming or cutting back. Other than that I only collect leaves if they have fallen from the plant. If you are stuck then you could pick a leaf from the plant or tree, but please ask permission first.

We probably all used dried leaves from herbs in our cooking, but I use all sorts of leaves in my magical workings. I use leaves from almost every type of plant and tree. As an example the blackberry is packed full of magical properties, but it is a bit squishy to use in spell work, unless you want the juice for a witch bottle of course because it does make a good 'blood' substitute. So, I collect and dry leaves from plants such as raspberries, blackberries and strawberries because they are easier to use in incense blends and magic pouches than the fruit.

If a leaf is big enough it can be used to write wishes and petitions on that can be sent away on the winds, buried in the earth, dropped into running water or burnt in the fire.

If you don't want to write on a leaf or you are out and about and don't have a pen with you, select a leaf and hold it in both hands then lift it up to your face and whisper your wish into it, fold it over and then allow the wind to take it away.

Bigger leaves make excellent wrappings for charms or spells that need to be buried or burnt, adding in the magical properties of the tree or plant to your spell work.

Leaves can also be melted onto candles, not only to make them look pretty, but also to bring their magic.

Look at a leaf; each one has a map, the thread of veins reaching out from the stem to the ends of the leaf and these pathways can be used as a guide for meditation, taking you on a journey.

And each leaf carries the magic of the tree and each tree has specific properties. Either ask the tree what energy it can lend to you or look up tree correspondences.

There is plenty of folklore, myths and magic linked to trees and some that are leaf-specific, such as:

- Make a circlet from fresh hazel leaves and wear to bring good luck, protection and to grant wishes.
- On a Friday after midnight in complete silence gather together nine holly leaves. Wrap the leaves up on a piece of white cloth using nine knots and tie the ends together. Place this under your pillow and your dreams will come true.
- The oracles at Delphi were said to chew on bay (laurel) leaves and inhale the smoke to help them receive visions.
- Laurel wreaths were worn for protection against the sky gods. Doctors also wore laurel leaves to protect against illness.
- Ancient kings wore crowns made from oak leaves as a symbol of the god they represented on earth.
- Rowan leaves and berries were carried to protect against witchcraft...and to keep the cows from being enchanted.
- Holly has a Christian connection in that it was said the leaves represented the thorns from Jesus' crown and the berries his drops of blood. However, it seems that this goes further back in time and relates to traditions in which a boy was selected from the village to wear a suit of holly leaves and a girl to wear a suit of ivy. They were then paraded around the village to bring nature and fertility to the dark part of the year.
- Holly leaves were also brought into the house to protect

against evil spirits and mischievous faeries.

- Hawthorn branches were cut for May Day, but only to decorate the outside of the house. To bring them inside was thought to bring illness and bad luck.
- Hawthorn leaves can be eaten and are often referred to as 'bread and cheese'.
- A sprig cut from the hawthorn that grows outside the St John's Church in Glastonbury is sent each year to the Queen.
- Burn hazel leaves for love and prosperity.
- Put ash leaves under your pillow to bring psychic dreams and visions.
- Put a bowl of water next to your bed and float some ash leaves in it to prevent illness.
- Place blackberry leaves around your home to return evil and bad luck to the person who sent them to you. It will also remove any unwanted spirits.

Seeds

The offspring of plants and trees, each one has the potential for new beginnings...

If you are out and about and you find seeds on the ground do collect one or two, but leave some for Mother Nature to do her thing. However, if there are plenty then they can be really useful in spell work.

For me any type of seed represents new beginnings of all kinds so they can be used in all sorts of spell working for new projects, new romance, new ideas, new outlooks...you get the idea.

Some seeds work particularly well for magic:

Acorns

Carry an acorn with you to bring luck, prosperity and protection.

Place an acorn on the windowsill under the full moon to bring money to you.

Plant an acorn under the light of a full moon to ensure luck and prosperity.

Bury an acorn on the dark moon to receive a quick infusion of money.

I have read in several articles that at Samhain witches gave each other acorns as gifts and that during the Burning Times giving someone an acorn was a secret way of letting them know you were a witch – how true these suggestions are I will leave up to you to research...

Use acorns in magical workings for fertility, strength, power and healing.

Keeping an acorn on your windowsill will apparently protect your home from lightning, according to folklore.

Wearing an acorn as a pendant is said to keep you young looking.

If you want to know whether your relationship is with your true love or not, you will need two acorn caps. Name one for yourself and one for your partner then float the caps in a bowl of water. If they float together then the relationship is blessed, if they float apart it might be time to pack your bags (or theirs).

When collecting acorns remember that not only do you need to leave enough for baby oaks to grow, but they are also food for lots of woodland creatures.

Carry an odd number of acorns in a green or red bag to keep good health.

Sycamore (Great Maple) Seeds

Helicopter seeds, as we used to call them when we were children, but I believe they are also called spinning jennies – whatever you call them they come with a heap load of magic.

Sycamore seeds bring harmony and energy, they banish tiredness and bring patience, prosperity, love, success, abundance and humility.

The seeds are excellent to use in any moon magic workings as they not only carry lunar energy, but also a huge feminine vibe.

Conkers/Horse Chestnut/Buckeye Seeds

We used to play 'conkers' in the school playground. With a horse chestnut seed hung on a piece of string, you tried to hit your opponent's conker; the loser was the one whose conker broke first. They are the shiny dark brown seeds that are found inside the bright green spiky outer shells from the horse chestnut tree.

Buckeye nuts found in the USA and conkers found in the UK are both nuts from horse chestnut trees and are incredibly similar to look at. Both trees, the American buckeye and the horse chestnut, belong to the same tree genus, *Aesculus*. Each has several different species, but they all produce very similar seeds, so the conker and the buckeye nut are interchangeable for magical purposes.

The conker/buckeye is brilliant for use in prosperity and money spells.

They are often carried in the pocket by gamblers to bring good luck and fortune.

Rub a conker/buckeye to bring good luck.

Wrap a monetary note around your conker/buckeye and put it in a magic pouch to bring prosperity.

To bring fertility, a gentleman could carry one in his pocket (it is said to resemble the shape of a testicle…).

Use conkers/buckeyes in magic pouches to bring fertility or to keep away evil.

Keep your conker/buckeye oiled and polished to keep the magic working.

Make a magic/medicine pouch from green fabric and add magical herbs and a conker/buckeye, then dress with money drawing oil for prosperity.

Carry a horse chestnut/buckeye with you to soothe and protect against arthritis.

For healing place a bowl of horse chestnuts in the person's room, wash the chestnuts daily in spring water to improve their ability to absorb the pain and illness from the patient, then dry them well. If a nut cracks or decays throw it out and replace it.

Note: Don't confuse the horse chestnut with sweet chestnut as conkers/buckeyes are very toxic in their raw state. One folklore story I found states that only half the buckeye is poisonous and that only squirrels know which half is safe in each nut...unless you are a squirrel, don't eat them...

Sweet Chestnuts

The sweet chestnut tree is *Castanea spp* from the *Fagaceae* family and also produces dark brown skinned seeds wrapped in spiky green cases similar to those of the horse chestnut, but smaller in size and they grow in clusters. They are also edible and rather scrummy roasted.

Sweet chestnuts can be used in magical workings for fertility much as the horse chestnuts are.

Keep sweet chestnuts in the house and also eat them to increase abundance.

Use sweet chestnuts in magical workings for energy, justice, success, grounding and centring and to increase your intuition.

Dandelion Seeds

Now we all know what a dandelion seed looks like, the pretty feathery seeds that float around on the summer breeze. I like to collect some of the seeds and keep them to use for wishes and wish spell workings. Don't collect all the seeds though, leave some to germinate because dandelions are a great source of pollen for bees.

Pop a dandelion seed into a witch bottle or magic pouch when creating a wishing spell.

If you have a full seed head blow the seeds completely to make your wish come true.

If you want to send a message to someone think about who and what then blow the seeds to send the message to them.

Think about your relationship with your partner, blow the seed head – if you blow all the seeds off in one breath then your relationship is good, if some seeds remain you may have to do some work...

Hazel Nut/Cob Nuts

The hazel nut (sometimes known as cob nut) comes from trees in the genus *Corylus*.

We are possibly more familiar with these nuts in a mixed bag at Yule time, but you can find hazel trees in the woodlands.

Use hazelnuts in magical workings for wisdom, divination, healing and creative inspiration.

Hang strings of hazel nuts in your home to attract the fae.

To get to the bottom of an issue crack a hazelnut and then meditate with it – the nutshell breaking symbolises 'cracking the situation open'.

The hazelnut is also vaguely heart shaped so it can be used in love magic.

The nutshell also symbolises the womb with the baby nut inside, which is where the fertility magic association comes from.

Catkins

Collect catkins from the hazel tree and wrap them in red ribbon or fabric. Charge them with the intent of strengthening your relationship with a loved one. Burn the bundle in the fire.

Rosehips

Rosehips are the fruit of the rose bush, but then that isn't a big surprise is it? If the rose blossoms are left on the plant and allowed to drop their petals, they will form a seed pod that is known as the rose hip.

As children, we would pick rosehips and split them open

to get the fibrous hairs from inside because it made excellent itching powder. However, it does have other more magical uses.

The rose is associated with the planet Venus and the element of water so it makes sense that they can be used in any love, friendship or peace workings.

Add rosehips to pot pourri to bring peace and calm to your house. Drop rosehips into a ritual bath or add to medicine pouches and charm bags. You can also pop them in incense blends.

With the element of water present, rosehips can be used in cleansing rituals or baths and can be added to witch bottles or medicine pouches to bring healing.

If you feel the need to draw love into your life you can work a rosehip love spell. String rose hips with a needle and thread to create a necklace. Charge the necklace with your intent to send energy out into the universe to draw a perfect mate to yourself. Don't be specific as the universe usually knows what is best for you, often better than you do yourself. Wear or carry your necklace with you when you go out.

Rose hip tea with a drop of honey can be shared with your beloved one to inspire the beginnings of a romantic evening... oooh la la...

Place rosehips around your home to bring harmony and peace, especially if there have been recent arguments. It will clear the air. Tuck them into drawers and cupboards or on windowsills and the top of door frames.

Sticks and Twigs

If you are looking for sticks or twigs to use then I would recommend you look on the ground first rather than cut them direct from the tree. The trees usually provide enough twiggy gifts without the need for cutting. However, if you do need to cut a twig or small branch from a tree, please do ask permission first. Just let the tree know what you need it for and always cut cleanly, never rip it from the tree otherwise infection can set in.

Twigs can be made into all sorts of magical items from the obvious handmade wand to twig crafts or a fetish. Twigs can also be burnt in ceremonial or magical fires, bringing the properties of each tree species to your working.

- Weave twigs into a crown or circlet and wear to impart the magical properties of the tree.
- Put hazel twigs on your windowsill to bring protection from storms to your house.
- Hang three hazel twigs tied together on the side of your house to protect against fire. Use small Y-shaped branches for divination.
- Burn ash logs at Yule to receive prosperity over the coming year. Wearing ash bark is said to protect against powerful magic.
- If your child is poorly get them to climb through the split in the trunk of an ash tree to bring healing.
- Ash wood makes good broom handles and wands because of its strength and protective properties.
- Make an amulet from ash twigs to bring out the healing solar energy; tie two small ash twigs together into an equal-armed cross, fasten in the centre with gold or yellow ribbon, charge the amulet in the sun.
- Carve a wish into a beech stick then bury it in the ground to make your wish come true.
- Use a wand made from beech wood to connect with spirit and the divine. Carry small pieces of beech bark with you for luck and success.
- Grind up a small piece of beech wood and pop the powder into your right shoe to bring good fortune.
- Use birch bark in protection spells. Birch wood works well for Yule logs and birch twigs are excellent for lighting Beltane fires. Birch twigs are traditionally used for making

a witch's broom.
- Dry out pieces of birch bark and use them to write spells on.

Journal Prompt

Make a note of any leaves, seeds or twigs that you collect, where they were found and what you used them for. Detail any magical workings and how well the results worked.

Nature's Mandala Wheel

I don't really have a proper name for this type of creation – power wheel, medicine wheel, mandala...you may feel the need to call it something completely different, but whatever the name of it is, this wheel is a powerful source of energy to be directed to whatever intent you have. It is like a big visual spell.

I like to start with a central feature, whether it is a crystal, a pebble, a candle or a tarot card of some sort – it gives the focus of intent. I then fan out in circles (or you could spiral it) using whatever I am drawn to use. If your intent is to bring things towards you (money, love, luck etc) then place the items in the circle in a deosil (clockwise) way, if you want to get rid of something (bad habits, negativity etc) then place the items in a pattern widdershins (anti-clockwise).

You can use all natural items such as pebbles, shells, leaves, sticks and flowers if you want to keep it totally wild. However, you can add in crystals or tarot and oracle cards if you like to use them.

Be creative and go with what works for you!

I leave the wheel creations in place for as long as feels necessary. Sometimes the wind will blow the parts around as I usually create my wheels in the conservatory, so during the summer the doors are open. Once the wind has done its work it usually feels like the right time to dismantle it. Otherwise it gets left alone until I feel the wheel has done the work required.

If I have used cards and crystals, they get cleansed and put away. The rest gets put into the compost bin, recycling or buried. Never leave anything outside that won't degrade properly.

Journal Prompt

Take photographs of any wheels you create, detail what you used to make them and why and of course what the results were.

Chapter 9

Roots

The roots of a plant hold an immense amount of magical power and have a connection to earth magic as well because they spend their entire life under the soil.

The roots of most plants can be dried and used in any kind of spell work just as you would use the dried leaves or flowers, but there are some that work particularly well from the root. As with any plant, check first whether the roots are toxic or need to be handled with care.

Roots, if they are big enough, can also have symbols and sigils carved into them.

Mandrake

The mandrake plant has a fabulous myth associated with it in that when the plant is pulled from the ground the root was thought to scream so loudly that anyone who was not prepared with ears full of wax would die an agonising death from the sound. The roots of the mandrake also grow in a bizarrely human body-like form so actually they make very good poppets. The mandrake was once thought to grow under hanged men, the plant being created as a result of the dripping fat, blood and semen that fell to the ground below the hanged body...

Legend says that if you want to pull a mandrake safely from the ground you should tie a hungry dog to the plant, plug your ears with wax and back away; the dog will follow you and pull the plant from the ground. Sadly this results in the dog dying from the screams, but the human presumably is fine.

I would not advise eating mandrake as it is part of the deadly nightshade family and in quantity it can have rather unpleasant results. However, the ancient Greeks used it as anaesthetic for surgery, but also steeped the root in wine for an aphrodisiac. During the Middle Ages mandrake was used to increase fertility; because the plant looked like a body a small mandrake root resembling a 'baby' was placed under the pillow. The root was also carried to bring good luck, prosperity and power. All this history and mythology makes the root extremely useful today for its magical properties of fertility, sleep, luck, prosperity and power.

John the Conqueror

John the Conqueror is perhaps one of the most well known roots used in magic. It is used primarily for luck, power and male fertility. The root can be steeped in oil to make anointing oil or ground to use in sachet (magic) powders or added to incense or washes. There are three types of John the Conqueror root; High John the Conqueror is the root/tuber of the *Ipomoea jalapa* and is the one most commonly used in magical workings. Low John root (sometimes called Dixie John or Southern John) is the root of the *Trillium grandiflora* and is used in some medicinal remedies, but is also carried for the magical properties of love or family. The third is Little John (or Chewing John), which is the root from the *Alpina galangal* (or Galangal) and is a member of the ginger family. It is chewed and the juice swallowed, leaving you with the mashed up bits of root to spit out. It is often used for justice and legal matters, the mashed root being spat on the courtroom floor. The root can also be dried and ground to use in candle magic.

Wrap a piece of John the Conqueror root and a silver coin in a paper money note to draw money to you, boost the magic by anointing with an oil blend or wrapping it in red or green material.

Pop a piece of John the Conqueror root in a piece of green or red material and add in a lodestone or magnet to create a love attraction pouch.

Liquorice Root

This brings back memories of my childhood when my father would buy us liquorice roots to chew on, presumably to keep us quiet for five minutes. It tastes of liquorice obviously, but doesn't have the sugary sweet flavour that we are perhaps used to from candy liquorice. Liquorice root used in magic brings power and the ability to change the wills and minds of others... not that I am suggesting you use it for this purpose, but it is always useful to know just in case.

Angelica Root

Sometimes known as Holy Ghost Root or Dong Quai, the angelica root is packed full of female power and strength and works very well in magical spells to protect children.

Burdock Root

I remember drinking dandelion and burdock fizzy drink as a child and loving it, I tried it again recently and thought it tasted like cough medicine... However, burdock root is excellent for cleansing and protection magic and works brilliantly to un-hex or un-cross.

Comfrey Root

Carry comfrey root with you to keep you safe while you travel.

Dandelion Root

Can be dried and steeped to make herbal tea or popped into a medicine pouch to bring you prophetic dreams and enhance your psychic abilities.

Golden Seal Root

This is an excellent root to use for wisdom and beauty magic, but also works well to increase your strength and general health.

Orris Root/Queen Elizabeth Root

This particular root is often used to attract men to you and can also be used to help make them fall in love with you. However, that is not something I would personally advise if you are targeting a specific individual, because that kind of magic opens up a whole host of problems, but it does work well in general 'bring love to me' workings too. However, the choice is yours...

Lovage Root

Bring on the love...lovage root attracts love, romance and passion...va va voom!

Ginger

Ginger brings a whole host of magical properties, which include healing, power, love, passion, success, prosperity, protection. I have also used ginger root as a substitute for High John the Conqueror when I haven't had any to hand.

Valerian Root

This one is on the darker side and is used for raising dark spirits and working any kind of black magic, but it is also used in making pacts.

Vegetables

Don't forget that vegetables are also roots and they can be used in all kinds of magical workings. Potatoes and carrots make excellent poppets and carrots and parsnips are slightly phallic shaped so make good roots to use in fertility spells. You can eat the vegetables with your meal to impart their special powers or you can slice them thinly and dry them out to grind or chop to use in incense blends, magical powders or candle magic.

The magical properties:

Beetroot: Passion, love, beauty and grounding.

Carrot: Clarity, fertility and passion.

Garlic: Healing, protection, hex breaking, lust, strength, courage, depression and negative energies.

Horseradish: Protection, energy, purification and passion.

Onion: Passion and fertility.

Parsnip: Male energy and sex magic.

Potato: Energy, magic, grounding, prosperity and healing.

Radish: Protection, passion and happiness.

Sweet potato: Love and passion.

Turnip: Protection.

Roots in general

Don't be limited to just using the roots I have listed above. Investigate and try out other plants and weeds. Experiment with the plant roots that you find when you are out and about or those that you have in your garden. What works for one person may not work so well for another. You may well find and create your very own unique and individual tool kit of magical roots; in fact I urge you to do just that.

Journal Prompt

Detail any roots that you use and where you found them growing, also how you worked with them and what the results were.

Chapter 10

Blossom, Berries, Mushrooms and Thorns

Blossom and Flowers

The blossom or flowers from any tree or plant can be popped into a vase to dress up your altar or dried or pressed to use in magical workings, incense blends and crafts. Dried petals and flowers can also be pressed onto candles quite effectively or steeped in oil to create anointing oils and perfumes.

For a more comprehensive list of plant and flower properties see my book *A Kitchen Witch's World of Magical Plants and Herbs* (shameless plug), but here are some of those often found in the wild:

Agrimony: Dispels negativity, reverses spells, aids spiritual healing, cleanses the aura, brings sleep, happiness, luck, love and protection.

Alexanders: Sea magic, intuition, emotions, cleansing and releasing.

Apple blossom: Love, healing and apparently immortality, but don't quote me on the last one...

Betony (wood): Love, purification, clarity, protection, anti-intoxication, nightmares, anti-depression, memory and stress relief.

Borage: Peace, courage, psychic powers, protection and happiness.

Broom: Purification, protection, luck and wind spell work.

Buttercup: Abundance, ancient wisdom, divination, protection and psychic abilities.

Celandine: Happiness, protection, release, escape and legal matters.

Chickweed: Love, fidelity, dreams, protection, fertility and moon magic.

Clover: Luck, money, protection, love, fidelity, exorcism and success.

Comfrey: Money, travel, protection, healing, hex breaking and bringing together.

Cowslip: Healing, peace, calm, treasure, youth and anti-visitor.

Daisy: Love, lust, protection, happiness, dreams, strength and courage.

Dandelion: Wishes, divination, love, abundance and psychic powers.

Elderflower: Protection, healing, faeries, purification, intuition, exorcism, hex breaking and rebirth.

Feverfew: Protection, peace, health and purification.

Foxglove: Protection, gossip, faeries and divination.

Gorse: Money and protection.

Hawthorn: Happiness, fertility, love, protection, purification, forgiveness, faeries and hope.

Heather: Luck, protection, cleansing, ghosts, rain, spirit, love, friendship, faeries, dreams and shape-shifting.

Meadowsweet: Peace, happiness and love.

Pennyroyal: Strength, protection, peace, initiation, goddess and business.

Primrose: Love, protection, faeries, changes and growth.

Self-heal/all heal: Releasing, cleansing, spirituality, stress, calming, clarity and protection.

Thistle: Protection, healing, exorcism, hex breaking and spirit.

Woodruff: Protection, money, balance and justice.

Yarrow: Psychic powers, love, courage, exorcism, dreams, peace, happiness, divination and protection.

Journal Prompt
Keep a record of any blooms that you find locally or use from

your garden, when they flower and how well they keep or how you dry them. Also, detail what you use them for and how well it works.

Berries

Berries can be dried to use in magical spell work or the edible ones can be used in cooking for magical purpose too. Make sure to leave some behind when you collect berries as the plant needs to pro-create and birds and animals eat most berries to keep them going through the cold months.

Berries can be dried laid out on a tray or they can be strung onto a thread using a needle and hung up to dry. The dried berries can then be used whole in magical workings and incense blends or ground to a powder.

Blackberry

The blackberry bramble grows all over the place and is extremely tough and hard wearing as I discovered when one seeded itself in the corner of my garden. They are really difficult to get rid of if you don't want them.

Folk believed that blackberries had healing powers and anyone suffering from something like boils or rheumatism would be dragged through arches of brambles to apparently bring about a cure...sounds incredibly painful to me.

Sleeping Beauty had her own bramble forest. The plant does grow very quickly and her castle was indeed covered in no time.

Ancient herbalists would use decoctions made from the leaves, roots and stems for any number of ailments from sore throats to diarrhoea and piles and the leaves would be used for dressings to put on burns and scalds.

I think blackberries are a sure sign that autumn is on the way. The blackberry plant is representative of earth, the leaves water and the thorns are fire, so it is a good all-round fruit. Because the plant produces fruit with lots of seeds and as the plant grows very quickly it is a really good fruit to use in prosperity or fertility spell work. The thorns can be carefully removed and added to protection pouches or witch bottles.

For magical spell work I would suggest drying the leaves or the roots because using the actual fruit makes an incredible mess. Unless you are looking for something to represent blood, then the juice works incredibly well as a substitute. The inhabitants of Faerie also love blackberries.

Elderberries

Elder is a small deciduous tree (or shrub) that grows in woods, hedgerows and on waste ground. The trunk is quite often crooked and low-lying with rugged bark. It has dark green leaves that have quite an unpleasant smell, but the flowers that appear in early summer are pretty and fragrant with large flat bunches of white blossom that ripens into berries. These are green at first and then a dark purple colour by early autumn.

Described in the past as a 'whole medicine chest' in one tree, the elder is an excellent ingredient to use in healing spell work.

The stem was said to have been used by Prometheus to bring fire to man from the gods.

It is also a tree of the Fae; sit and watch patiently on midsummer night and you should see the Faerie King ride past...if you are lucky.

If an elder self-seeds in your garden it is said that the Earth Mother has chosen to protect your house (don't cut the elder down without asking permission from the Earth Mother first). Preferably, of course, don't cut any trees down at all.

There has been a bit of a dilemma with elder over the years. It has been a tree of life, but also a tree of the devil; it was needed for its medicinal properties, but also feared to be a witches' plant – sometimes you just can't win! Witches were said to be able to turn themselves into elder trees...I have yet to attempt it.

A tree of death, rebirth and reincarnation. The bark, root,

leaves and berries can be used for making dyes.

Use in any healing spell work, whether it is for physical or emotional healing. It is also very good to use to break spells that were cast against you. Elder wands can be used to drive out evil spirits.

Drink elderberry juice to increase your intuition. Add elderberry tea to your bath water to help heal spiritual and emotional issues.

Add elder stems to incense blends to bring purification and protection to your home.

Hawthorn

Hawthorn is a hedgerow plant that grows well even in poor soil and high winds. It has white flowers in spring that are followed by dark red berries in the autumn. Watch out for the spiky thorns though.

Associated with easing heart complaints, I think it works well in love workings and spells to make the heart sing with happiness (awwwwww).

Hawthorn is a tree of the Fae. Forming the Faerie triad with oak and ash, the hawthorn offers a gateway to the world of Faerie.

The white flowers followed by the red berries have long been associated with fertility.

Dry hawthorn berries and thread onto black cotton then hang them above your threshold or sprinkle the berries around the boundary to your home for protection.

Add hawthorn berries to your floor wash to purify your house. Hawthorn berries can be sprinkled around your home to protect your marriage or relationship.

Add to workings where you require forgiveness.

Use hawthorn in workings for protection, hope and warding against evil...yes, another tree that protects against witches, *sigh*, although apparently witches would shape-shift into hawthorn trees to rest before flying through the night.

Holly

Holly is an evergreen shrub that can grow into a tree if left to its own devices. Holly has dark glossy green leaves and red berries during winter. It wouldn't be Yule without holly would it? However, holly is also burnt at Imbolc ceremonies.

Keep a sprig of holly above your bed to ensure good dreams and insightful visions.

Plant holly around your property for protection against lightning, poison and evil spirits.

Put holly sprigs on your altar at the winter solstice to invite happiness, balance, success and luck into your life for the coming year.

The holly berry is symbolic of the life-giving blood of the Goddess; to work with fertility and feminine sexuality take three holly berries and throw them in water (the ocean, a river or a pond) and make your request to deity as you do so.

Juniper

Juniper is an evergreen shrub that can spread or grow upright depending on location. It has short, spiny-tipped leaves and yellow flowers in early summer, which turn into green berry cones that then ripen to the dark purple juniper berries we are familiar with.

This is another herb that is old as the hills, dating back to Neolithic times apparently (personally I don't remember that far back).

Keep a sprig of juniper above the door for protection and to keep negative energy out. It has very strong protective properties that keep out all sorts of evil demons.

If you have had something stolen, you can petition the spirit of the juniper bush to bring the article back to you and justice to be served.

Wear juniper berries in an amulet to bring love to you and to keep you healthy; also use in healing workings.

Use in incense blends to purify and cleanse, bring clarity and also to aid with psychic powers. Juniper has strong connections to the spirit world and the afterlife.

Juniper also works well in moon magic, on the dark of the moon.

Mushrooms

We shall focus here on the edible fungi variety as opposed to the hallucinogenic mushrooms...

You can forage for many types of mushroom in the wild, but please make sure you have identified it correctly as there are a lot of poisonous varieties that could make you very sick...or worse...

Mushrooms can be eaten to gain strength and courage. I think this stems from the belief that the mushroom is a vegetable substitute for 'flesh' given its texture.

The fact that quite often mushrooms seem to appear magically overnight and they are frequently found as a Faerie ring entitles them to a bit of magic and mysticism.

They are an interesting food, as they have the feminine energy of the moon, but also the grounding energy of the earth, bringing about a good balance.

Journal Prompt

Keep a record of any berries that you find locally. Note where and when you found them and how you dried or stored them. Detail any magical workings that you used them for. Also, keep a record of what mushrooms you found and where. It may also help to keep photos of mushrooms to help with future identification.

Thorns

Lots of plants have thorns on them; roses, brambles and blackthorn spring to mind and these thorns can be used for magic. Think about what a thorn does. They are protection for the plant, they guard it against predators and they are sharp and defensive. They can pierce, they can cut and they can draw blood.

Folklore says that blackthorn thorns were always used to curse, but folklore says a lot of things that we have since twisted around to our advantage. If that is the choice you make...thorns (any type) are very good for cursing and hexing spell work. Rose thorns work especially well in affairs of a broken heart.

A blackthorn wand with the thorns on is sometimes referred to as a 'black rod' and used in darker magic to cause harm to others. In medieval times it was believed that the Devil pricked the fingers of his followers with thorns from the blackthorn tree.

But thorns also have a positive side and can be used in spell workings for protection and to dispel negative energy.

Long thorns such as those of the blackthorn can be used instead of pins to stick into poppets and also used to carve symbols into candles. Don't forget poppets can be used for all kinds of intent, not just hexing. They can also be used for healing, love, friendship, protection or whatever use you want really.

Use thorns dipped in ink to write magical petitions or 'fix' magical workings.

Use thorns in magic to 'pierce' negative bubbles and break bad cycles that you have gotten into.

Thorn Protection

Gather together three, six or nine thorns (be guided by your intuition) from the plant of your choice (blackthorn works well for this as it already carries the energy of protection in the tree itself) then write the name of the person you need protection from or the feeling such as 'jealousy' on a small piece of paper then wrap it around the thorns. Bury the 'working' under the tree itself if that is possible, if not bury it in the ground (at a crossroads works well too) or failing that burn it.

Return to Sender Thorn Spell

If you are getting grief from someone and have just about had enough, this spell will work to send the negative energy back to the original source. This isn't meant to cause harm to the person in question, just deflect what they have sent out to you back towards them. Be careful with this one though, think it through first and do not work this magic while angry otherwise it could go horribly wrong...

Using a candle or a poppet (this can be as simple as a potato) to represent the person. You will also need three long thorns. Push each thorn into the poppet/candle; one at the top, one in the heart position and one in the middle (head, heart, stomach). Light the candle and then visualise a protective barrier around yourself that looks like mirrors and see the negative energy and ill wishes reflecting back to the person that sent them. You might like to create a chant to say as well. Allow the candle to burn completely and when it is done visualise cutting yourself off from the person, removing all ties and connections. Bury the leftover spell items.

Thorn Healing

You can work a similar poppet or candle spell as above, but use it for healing. Stick the thorn into the poppet or candle in the position on the 'body' that the person needs healing. So, for instance, if the person has a headache you stick the thorn in the top of the candle or the head of the poppet. Visualise healing energy coming from Mother Earth/the Universe and being directed through the point of the thorn into the body.

Journal Prompt

Keep a record of any thorns that you collect and how you used them.

Chapter 11

Feathers and Fetishes

I am always being gifted with feathers; when I am in town usually pigeon ones, but I have also been given crow and magpie ones too. If you are in the forest you may find all sorts of bird feathers and on the beach it will probably be seagull feathers. Whatever kinds they are, feathers carry their own very special magic with them.

When I find a feather I usually take it home and pop it in the freezer overnight, just as a precaution really because the cold temperature will get rid of any nasties that might be lurking therein. Obviously keep the feather away from your frozen food! Alternatively you can place feathers in a solution of five parts warm water, one part vinegar and one part witch hazel, leave them to soak for 24 hours then dry them by laying them out flat on a towel.

Feathers bring the magical properties of change, focus, communication, concentration and wishes. But the feather will also carry the magical energies of the specific bird it came from and the colour of the feather will mean something too.

- Blue jay feathers bring joy, happiness and light.
- Crow feathers are excellent for wisdom, knowledge and helping us to let go of unwanted feelings, thoughts or negative energy.
- Robin feathers bring new projects, plans and beginnings.
- White swan feathers hold purification, cleansing, beauty and positive energy and black swan feathers can be used to dispel negative energy.
- Hawk feathers bring the magic of the hunt.
- Eagle feathers hold huge amounts of energy, but also

bring peace, happiness and protection.

- Magpie feathers bring magic, divination skills, wisdom and change.
- Pigeon feathers bring peace, love and communication.
- Blackbird feathers bring poetry, inspiration, music and a stronger connection with meditation.
- White feathers found in your pathway are said to be messages from the Divine, spirit or angels.

I was lucky enough to have been gifted a whole magpie wing, which is one of my totem animals so it sits on my altar. If you do find a road kill bird and are not squeamish you can honour the animal by using it for magic. If the thought of it makes your stomach churn then you can also honour the animal by moving it to the verge or hedgerow so that nature can do what it does best and the animal will be returned to the earth and probably feed a crow or two as well. I have skinned a rabbit (for dinner), plucked a pheasant and deboned a chicken, but preparing a bird for preservation is a whole other level of ick…be prepared.

For any animal or bird remains that I stumble across, whether they can be used for preserving or not, I think it is a nice idea to give a blessing for the animal and the life that it has had; just a few words said to the earth or the sky, thanking the animal for its part in the cycle of life.

In the late 1800s in the eaves of a house in England some strange items were discovered. They consisted of a chair, four brooms and a string of feathers. It was declared that the house had belonged to a witch as the chair was for sitting in, the brooms had been used for flying and the string of feathers was referred to as a 'witches' ladder'. The witches' ladder was a long string made from cockerel feathers and it was suggested that it might have been used by the witch to cross over the roof, to cause deaths and to hex the neighbour's cattle. A second string of feathers was also found, which had much newer feathers in it.

Then a third was found, which had feathers bound loosely to a skein of black wool.

At the time it was said that each feather was a hex, a curse or a bad wish, the witches' ladder would then be thrown into a pool of water where the feathers would eventually pull away from the wool releasing the curses, these would appear on the surface of the water as bubbles.

You could create a witches' ladder with twine, wool or ribbon and insert feathers for a curse, but equally you can also create witches' ladders for positive intent such as luck, prosperity, love, healing or success. Insert a feather for each wish.

During the First World War a group of women formed the White Feather Society and they would present a white feather to any man who would not join the military and fight – showing him that they believed him to be a coward. This apparently came from cock fights where a cockerel with white tail feathers would turn away from their opponent and show their white tail feathers during the fight and were considered to be cowardly.

If you were a sailor and wanted to protect yourself against being shipwrecked you would find yourself a wren, catch and kill it on Christmas Eve then tie it on the top of a pole with its wings outstretched. You would carry it around town, allowing other sailors to purchase a feather in exchange for a coin. At the end of the day the wren would be buried on the seashore and the sailors would keep the feathers with them as good luck talismans.

It is said that sewing the feather from a swan into your husband's pillow will keep him faithful.

Pigeon feathers added to your bed or pillow will supposedly prolong the pain and agony for someone who is dying. Yes, that does say 'prolong', meaning that you wish to make the illness last much longer than it should.

Preserving bird parts

There are a lot of tutorials online. Google 'how to preserve bird wings' and you will get some very good details. A lot of the guides suggest popping the animal part in the freezer for a couple of weeks first to kill any insect eggs. Essentially you need to cut the wing, head or legs off with a hacksaw or very sharp cutters. Then the item can be placed in a box on a thick layer of cornmeal or borax. Pour more cornmeal, rock salt or borax over the top so that it is completely covered, then put the lid on the box, making a few slits in the lid to allow for air. Place the box in a dark, dry storage area for about a month. If it starts to smell bad then it has spoiled. When the items are completely dry, use a small, soft brush to clean the cornmeal way from the feathers.

The basic guidelines for if you find a dead bird and want to preserve it are:

- If it has insects or maggots crawling on it then it won't be any good for preserving, leave it for nature.
- If the carcass smells bad, leave it for the worms.
- Leave the parts for as long as they need; they will be fully preserved when they feel dry and completely stiff. If any bits are sticky or damp, leave them for longer. Wings as a general guide take at least a month to dry out properly.
- If you just want to use the feathers pluck them away from the body gently and carefully.
- Check the laws of your particular country before you go claiming any bird. In some countries it is illegal to possess parts from birds of prey without special permits.
- Dry the parts indoors at room temperature in a dry place; don't leave the items outside as changes in humidity and temperature are not helpful.

Journal Prompt

Make a note of any feathers that are gifted to you, when and where they arrived and from what bird they came. Also, keep a note of how you used them.

It's a Fetish Thing...

No...not *that* kind of fetish...

The word 'fetish' possibly originates from a Portuguese word 'feitico' meaning charm or sorcery, so essentially it is an item filled with magic and you will find versions of them in most cultures.

A fetish can be an object that has a connection to the supernatural with the item representing the divine or spirit world or some have a spirit that resides within the fetish. Other fetishes are natural objects or any items that have been imbued with magical intent.

A fetish is designed and carried or worn to bring protection, love, prosperity or luck and to protect against evil although some are created to bring curses upon enemies.

A fetish can be anything such as a poppet, carved images, animal bones, an ornament or a pouch filled with herbs and other more unsavoury ingredients (think bodily fluids...). I usually like to use feathers, leaves, twigs and stones as types of fetishes.

If you like the idea of trapping a spirit and binding it into an object then I would suggest you do some serious research first... it is not something to be done without great care and thought and I would suggest only a very experienced practitioner attempt it. The spirit you bind into your fetish may have a completely different idea to you of what is right and wrong and it could be incredibly unreliable – hey it is has been bound against its will and trapped in an ornament...how would you feel? Some spirit-filled fetishes can be dangerous and very, very draining on your own energy. A fetish may also need to be completely dominated before it will do any kind of bidding.

However, not wishing to be a complete drama queen about it, some spirits will step into an object of their own free will,

possibly enjoying the whole 'being worshipped as a god' idea...
be warned, be careful, trust your intuition, do your homework...

Making your own fetish is advisable, rather than buying one.
It will have more power and be personal to you, but it doesn't
have to be complicated, it can just be a pebble.

Your fetish will need to be activated and by that I mean you
will need to imbue it with your magical intent or the energy of
the deity or spirit that you want it to have or, sometimes if it is a
natural item, it may need activating to release the energy of the
spirit that is already within it. (Every natural item has its own
spirit energy.) Once your fetish is set up it is essentially a 'living
thing' and will need attention and even feeding.

In hoodoo magic you can make a fetish mojo bag that you fill
with items corresponding to your intent and once it is activated you
regularly feed it with a magic powder to keep the powers working.

You can soak your item in oils or scented water, pass it
through incense smoke or add corresponding herbs. If you are
dedicating it to a particular deity, use items that are associated
with them.

Get creative...bones, paintings, images, spirit bottles, witches'
bottles, witches' ladders, statues, dolls, poppets, beaded cloth,
pebbles, twigs, feathers...the material choice is endless.

All the time you pay your fetish attention and keep feeding
the energy it will keep working for you.

If you haven't worked with the spirit world before I would
suggest you try the basic magical intent fetish first and just
activate the natural spirit of the item rather than trapping an
unwilling spirit...it saves having to scrape ectoplasm off the
walls...

Journal Prompt
Make a note and even keep a photograph of any fetishes you
make, what you used, what the intent was for and how it worked
out.

Chapter 12

Curses, Hexes, Bindings and Banishings

Curses and Hexes

Knowledge is power and if you know about curses and hexes then you are fore warned and fore armed. If you choose to hex or curse then that of course is your right to do so, just be mindful of any possible backlash...

I am also not going to get on a soap box and spout off about morals, taking the high ground, talking about karma and so on – that choice is yours to make, and yours alone.

My personal thoughts are if you get cross or upset about something or with someone...stop...think... Don't just blindly work a spell to curse or hex someone in the heat of anger. Let the hurt die down first, and then decide what course of action to take.

Sometimes there are situations that warrant some kind of action or reaction and sometimes it is not easy to decide what course to follow. A good rule of thumb is if you would not do it physically then don't do it magically. Make sure that what you do, whatever kind of defensive action you take, is equivalent to the action that was taken against you. You would not blow up someone's car just for stepping on your toe would you? Think about your plan of action; if you feel uncomfortable in any way then don't do it, go back to the drawing board and come up with Plan B, C or D (and all the rest of the letters in the alphabet if need be).

Curses and hexes are not for the faint-hearted. If you decide that is the path you want to go down, I urge you to not take them lightly and never chuck them about willy nilly – take responsibility for your actions. You also need to be very, very sure that the person you are sending a curse or hex to was the person responsible in the first place…

Now the lecture has been delivered let's take a look at what hexes and curses are.

Just as there are hundreds and thousands of love and prosperity spells, there are probably as many for hexes. Some of them involve long, complicated rituals; some require all sorts of ingredients and some are just gestures with a hand or a word.

So, what is the difference between a hex and a curse? Well I am not sure there is much of a difference to be honest, just different names from different cultures. However, the general consensus seems to be that a hex is a spell or bewitchment. Traditionally they could be good or bad and a witch would be paid to provide one. A curse is a malevolent spell that is cast with the purpose of inflicting harm upon another; curses can be spoken or written. Objects can also be cursed with bad luck, misfortune, ill health and even death.

Essentially, it is the wilful direction of negative energy towards someone with the intent to harm. Usually hexes and curses take some time to develop, building up slowly. However, if you are well shielded and protected you are very unlikely to become the victim of a hex yourself and I think it happens a lot less frequently than people believe.

Cursing Stones

Charging a stone with malevolence is an ancient method of delivering a curse.

This is done when you are feeling full of negative emotions such as rage, anger and hatred; you direct all those emotions into the stone. It can then be stored and used later by taking up the stone in your hands, turning it widdershins and directing those emotions to where you want them to go.

(Also, a useful way of venting any anger and frustration by sending it into the stone, you could then drop it into the sea or a river so that those negative emotions wash away.)

To curse someone, hold the stone in your hand, stroking it while turning it widdershins and saying your curse.

Binding

I would like to also look at binding. This is a form of spell that binds a person or situation so that they/it can no longer harm you. I have found this form of working particularly successful. As long as you are pure in your intent, it doesn't actually harm the person or cause them any discomfort, it just stops them from hurting or harassing you. But bear in mind that this spell does take away the free will of the person you are binding, so use with caution.

A binding spell can be very simple – you use an object that represents the person causing you harm – it can be a poppet, it could be a photograph or it could just be a lump of clay that you have identified as the person. It can then be bound with string, ribbon, ivy or I have found that sticky tape works extremely well. As you bind the object visualise binding the harmful energies of that person and speak your wishes, that the person can no longer harm you or harass you. Bury the spell.

Banishing

And on to banishing. I have had a lot of experience with this and not all of it has been good. When I first started on this pathway I thought it sounded like a lovely idea to 'banish negative energy' from my life. What I didn't expect was the huge circle that this banishing covers. It does not just get rid of bad luck it covers all sorts of things...including people. To banish all negative energy from your life is not always a good thing. We all need a balance in life. For instance, think about batteries – they need positive and negative to work, and if you took away the negative they would have no power.

It is much better to ask that 'any negative energy that serves me no good' be released; it is safer believe me. Note I also used the word 'release' rather than 'banish', I have also found that is safer. But please be prepared for unexpected results...

Simple banishing spells can be worked with fruits or berries; an apple works well. Carve a symbol or word (or name) into the side of the apple that represents that which you wish to banish. Bury the apple in the ground and as it rots it will work the banishing magic.

Please remember that whatever you banish leaves a hole, that hole must be purposely filled with positive energy otherwise it will just be replaced with something similar to the thing you wanted to get rid of in the first place. And remember that banishing often takes time to work too.

Journal Prompt

I think it is a good idea to keep a record of any curses, hexes and the like because it helps to follow the trail and see how well they worked and how long they took to take effect and just in case there is any backlash you can see where it came from and why.

Chapter 13

Naturally Magical Objects

Soil and Earth

Dirt basically and it comes in many forms; some soil is light and sandy and others (like the stuff in my garden) is thick and clay-like. And all manner of types in between, but essentially it is full of magic. Soil is obviously aligned with the element of earth, but it holds a definite life force as it is jammed-pack full of nutrients to feed the plants.

Earth is grounding and solid, bringing stability and strength with it. It doesn't matter if you are standing knee deep in mud at a festival or on concrete paving in a shopping centre, the earth is there beneath your feet. Soil, earth, dirt, mud, graveyard dirt and clay are all different forms with the same source.

Soil can be used in all sorts of magical workings and as always go with your intuition, but I tend to use it for the following:

Magical properties: Fertility, nurturing, stabilising, grounding, manifestation, prosperity, employment, home, protection, rebirth.
Gender: Feminine.
Direction: North.
Elementals: Gnomes, dwarves, brownies.
Uses: Burying, planting, making mandalas and sigils.

Stones

You can find stones anywhere. It might be in the hedgerow, the forest, a field, on the seashore or in your garden. If you are really stuck then you can buy them in a bag at home depot stores.

Stones carry a huge amount of earth energy with them and they have all sorts of uses. If you are lucky enough to live by the sea or a river you may even find hag stones; sometimes called holey stones, hex stones or faerie stones. Basically they are stones where the water has worked through them and made a hole in the centre.

In folklore, hag stones were often used to ward against curses, nightmares, evil spirits and of course witches... They can also be used to look through to see into other worlds, realms or to see faeries. It is also said that you can look through the hole in a hag stone and see things clearly as it helps to look past any glamours or illusions.

These stones were used to keep away the evil hag spirit that would bring nightmares and so the stones were hung in bedrooms and placed on windowsills.

Some sailors would tie holey stones to the bows of their boats to protect against malevolent witchcraft. Similarly farm buildings would have a small holey stone or pebble tied to the key for the building – this was to prevent the witches that rode the hedgerows at night from hexing the farm and to prevent the witches from 'hag riding' the horses.

Wearing a hag stone around your neck as an amulet was said to protect the wearer against the evil eye and would also apparently prevent the wearer from being pixie led while out walking.

The holey stone was also said to be able to cure disease, either by wearing the stone as a pendant around the neck or by rubbing the stone over a wound or painful joint.

So...basically as I am assuming you don't want to use hag stones to protect against witches...they can be used for all sorts of protection and healing spell work. They can be worn as amulets or popped into medicine pouches or witch bottles. You can also just put them on your windowsills or hang one above your doorway for protection. If you are looking for a bit of fertility, they are also good to hang over your bed to help facilitate pregnancy.

If you happen to find several hag stones they can be strung on a piece of string, each one spaced apart and knotted below, this adds to the power of the stone by bringing knot magic into play as well.

Hold a hag stone in your left hand and visualise success and your desires; rub your thumb around the hole in the stone in a deosil direction. Keep the stone with you and repeat the spell regularly to reinforce the magic.

But...depending on where you live, hag stones aren't always easy to find so...use your intuition and pick pebbles or stones that appeal to you. Sometimes a nice looking stone will find its way to you. Each stone has the power of the element of earth so it can pack a good protection punch even if it hasn't got a hole in it.

If you have worries or troubles or feel that you need to get rid of some negative vibes then send them into a pebble or stone. Once you have released your woes into the stone, throw it into a river or the sea or bury it beneath the earth...taking your troubles away with it.

Flat pebbles can also be used to draw beautiful images on. I have several that I have used as god and goddess representations on my altar. I also mark the compass directions on large stones to use in ritual. You can draw images of animals on pebbles to use as animal spirit guide correspondences or just write positive affirmation words on pebbles to keep in the house to remind you to be happy.

If you manage to find a large flattish stone it can be used as a garden altar or for burning loose incense upon.

Journal Prompt

Keep a note of any pebbles or stones you collect and where they came from, it might prove useful if you come to use them in a working because you then have some of their history and can use that as a base for any magic.

Bones

In the past bones and animal parts were used widely for magical purpose. People were hunters, they used all the parts of an animal, primarily for food and warmth and the bones for magic.

Now I do not advocate anyone popping out and hitting a badger over the head with a stick just to use the bones in a spell. However, nature itself provides dead animals and birds and man in his motor car supplies a lot too. Picking up road kill may sound a bit yucky and is not for everyone or the faint-hearted, but I think of it as honouring the animal, that its skin and bones will be put to some good use after it has passed away.

The bones themselves are a good way of connecting with the spirit of the animal and working with those energies. I have a magpie skull on my altar as magpie is one of my animal totems; I put it on my altar in honour of the spirit. The bone of the animal works as a vessel for the spirit to reside in within our realm. Animal bones can also be carried in medicine bags to use their particular energies. All animal spirits take time to bond with, so don't rush it. It is also a nice idea to leave offerings for the animal bones you have found.

You can wear the bones to take on the attributes and power of the animal that they belonged to. A lot of animals are shamanic in nature, enabling you to tap into their ability to travel between worlds.

Feathers, animal skins or bones can also be used in shapeshifting. The skins can be worn and the feathers or bones used as jewellery to aid you in taking on the form of the animal.

Ritual tools can also be made from animal bones – rattles for instance, or tie bones to your staff or wand for an added energy boost.

Don't waste the bones from your Sunday dinner either; chicken bones especially make really good divination sets. And the bones can be used in your magical work.

Keep an eye out when you are walking through the woods

and fields because you do occasionally find small animal bones. I have one that I believe to be from a rabbit.

Antlers that have been naturally shed also make wonderful magical tools.

Also, don't forget about insects. They have bones – they just wear them on the outside. Watch for dead insects that can be used in magical workings. Please make sure they are dead first...

Bone Folklore

There is some fascinating folklore about using bones for magic. Here are some traditional folk beliefs:

- Carry the jawbone of a donkey in your teeth while walking backwards. This will cure a toothache (although I am pretty sure it would cause a toothache rather than cure one).
- Bite down on a white button made from bone to cure a headache or a toothache.
- Carry a bone from a hog's head in your pocket to prevent headaches.
- Hang the bones of a turkey vulture around your neck to prevent headaches.
- Powdered eagle bones are useful to cure headaches.
- Rub a dry bone over a wart then throw the bone away without looking back to get rid of the wart.
- To remove a birthmark, visit a cemetery before sunrise, find a human bone and rub this three times on your birthmark while saying the name of the Father, Son and Holy Ghost.
- To cure a tumour or abscess, take a human bone from a cemetery and rub it over the abscess or tumour then bury the bone under a waterspout of a roof where the sun or moon cannot shine upon it.
- Pulling the turkey wishbone is lucky for the one who gets

the larger part and they should place it over the kitchen door or in the closet for luck.

- Put a wishbone over your door on New Year's Day and the first person to enter the house will be your friend that year.
- A charm made from breast bones of kingfishers and jays with small holey stones keeps away evil spirits.
- Carrying the jaw or breast bone of a tree toad will bring you luck.
- Keep a turtle bone in your pocket for good luck.
- Carrying a bone from the body of a boiled black cat will make the carrier invisible.

NB. It goes without saying that you are not allowed to remove human bones from graveyards or kill eagles or boil black cats… just in case you thought about it.

Cleaning Bones

If you want to work with the bones from a road kill animal there are various ways of cleaning the them for use – do a search on Google for tutorials but below are the basics.

Clean as much of the flesh from the bones as you can, then the bones can be cleaned by popping them in a jar with fresh water. Put the lid on then leave it for two or three days, change the water for fresh, keep doing this until the flesh has all come away from the bones. You can also do the same thing using biological washing powder and warm water.

Drop the bones into a dish or jar and very carefully pour over a solution of hydrogen peroxide (the chemist has this or failing that purchase hair bleach, which is what I used on my magpie skull). Not only does this take the last bits of flesh away from the bone, it also bleaches it to a nice colour.

Or you can bury it…dig a shallow hole in the soil and bury the bones so that Mother Nature's worms and insects can do the cleaning job for you. This takes patience...and you also need to remember where you buried it.

Red Bones

Some cultures have taken to colouring bones with the colour red to create the image of blood and life energy within them. You can do this fairly easily; mix red wine and red ochre together to make a paste and leave it to sit covered in a bowl for a couple of days. If you can't get red ochre you can use red brick dust. Apply the paste to the cleaned bones making sure to cover them completely. Wrap the items in plastic to keep the paste moist. Leave for a further 24 hours. If the paste looks like it is drying out give it a spray with water. Remove the paste and allow the bones to dry. You may need to use a soft brush to remove any lingering paste. Don't wash the bones, just wipe them with a soft cloth.

Journal Prompt

Keep a record of any road kill or bones you find out in nature, where and when and how you cleaned and cleansed them. Make a note of what the animal or bird was for future reference.

Make it Personal

Another area of magic I would like to briefly mention here is about making spells and magic personal and by that, I mean fluids...of the bodily kind.

Now this is a subject that you will either find absolutely fascinating or you will skip quickly past this section. Either is absolutely okay. It is your pathway, your journey and therefore your choice about what you include or don't, but here it is just in case...

Your body is the vessel that carries the magic, the energy and the intent, but it is also unique and individual to you. So if you want to add the personal touch to any working you can literally add a bit of yourself into it. Or a bit of someone else…

If you are working magic for someone else or that involves someone else, for instance a healing poppet, you may want to add in something of theirs that will link the magical item to them. Let's suggest an easy option of a piece of hair or a nail clipping. The energy from the person will be in that very personal item collected from them.

Hair is often used as it is fairly easy to obtain and perhaps less intrusive than some of the other items. It can also be used like string or twine and work as a binding.

Nail clippings are another traditional personal item used in magic, even if it may involve rooting around in the bathroom waste bin to find what you need. I don't personally think they are quite as powerful as hair, but they do work well.

Menstrual blood is an ancient magical fluid and although obviously only obtainable from women of a certain age it carries an immense amount of power. This bodily fluid brings power, protection, love, passion, sexuality, fertility and lunar magic.

You can add menstrual blood to most magical workings to link in yourself or a particular person. It can also be used in love magic to bind someone to you (think very carefully about whether you really want to go down that route).

Menstrual blood can also be used to anoint your magical and divination tools to give them a strong connection to you.

To bring fertility bury a terracotta pot containing menstrual blood at the foot of a fertile tree and request blessings of the fertility kind from the tree. Ask nicely and remember to compliment the tree on how wonderful it looks.

Saliva – good ol' spit. There is a reason why spitting is so rude other than because it is a revolting habit. Saliva is actually thought to be quite controlling. It also brings the magical properties of protection and the ability to dispel negative spirits. Spit in the direction of a perceived threat to dispel negative energy. If you don't know what direction it is coming from, spit over your left shoulder. On the positive side, spit is also considered lucky and can transmit your will and intent. Spit on betting tickets or lottery cards to bring good fortune.

Sexual fluids from both males and females can also be used in much the same way as menstrual blood although they have a more vulnerable magic to them. Female fluids have very strong fertility and life power magic and male fluid is believed to have very good healing properties.

Sweat can be used. Although I am not sure how easy it is to actually collect droplets, you can wipe a cloth across a sweaty brow or armpit and this can be used in sex and love magic quite successfully although it does have a more masculine energy.

Urine – historically one of the most common ingredients found in witch bottles that were buried in walls and chimneys of old houses. Funnily enough, these were originally used to protect against witches. Your pee is obviously very personal to you and can be used in protection, territory and domination magic.

Journal Prompt

Make a note of any magical workings using bodily fluids, what you used and how well the result turned out.

Horseshoes

You may be lucky enough to find a horseshoe when you are out and about on your travels, but what is all the fuss about them?

There is a very big connection between horseshoes and the Faerie folk, horseshoes being made from iron and the fair folk having a great aversion to the stuff. The Faeries were blamed for all sorts of mishaps within the house such as things going missing, milk going sour and chickens not laying. To be honest, they probably were responsible for a great number of those things. The belief was spread that Faeries did not like iron and so apparently people started hanging iron horseshoes on their front doors as protection. The horseshoe not only has the protective quality of being iron, but it is also shaped like the moon, which also has power.

There are two schools of thought; one is that the horseshoe should be hung points upwards to stop the good luck from falling out and the second believe that the points should be downwards so that the luck pours out over those people walking through the doorway.

Another branch of folklore states that the horseshoe is a symbol of the moon goddess and hanging the horseshoe over your door brings blessings and protection from the goddess. There is also the suggestion that a horseshoe hung points downwards represented the feminine energy of the Irish goddess Sheela na Gig or the Christian Virgin Mary; the inference being that the horseshoe is shaped like a yoni...obviously, they had a lot of time on their hands to think about things...

The horseshoe is also hung over doorways points downwards so that no witch would be able to pass under it and enter the house.

In some cultures, the horseshoe is hung in the house and touched to bring luck and in Mexico there is a tradition of wrapping the horseshoe in coloured thread and decorating it with holy prints and a prayer.

The horseshoe shape as a symbol has been adopted for luck and is used in all manner of items such as jewellery to bring luck to gamblers particularly, but also because it is shaped somewhat like a magnet so it can be used to 'draw' money to you in magical workings.

There are many stories along the same theme about the blacksmith and the devil...the devil appearing inside a smithy one day and demanding that the blacksmith fit him with his own iron shoes. The blacksmith, realising that it was the devil, made a shoe and nailed it to the devil's hoof while it was still burning hot. The devil was in such pain that he ripped off the shoe and swore never to go back to a smithy again. Horseshoes were therefore hung over the entrance of a house to ward against the devil and any evil spirits.

The horseshoe was traditionally made from iron, which was the strongest known metal to our ancestors. It was also attached to the horse using seven nails, seven was thought to be a lucky number. Horses, of course, have their own power and strength and when walking on cobblestones the metal of the horse shoe could have thrown off sparks, which would have added to the magic. And iron itself would have been magical because it was taken from the earth and could withstand fire and cold so it would have been very highly regarded.

Iron is also associated with male sexual energy and carries a heap load of potent sex magic with it, think of the power and virility of a stallion...

Healing horseshoe: to relieve a headache hold a horseshoe against your forehead, visualise the pain leaving you and transferring into the horseshoe.

Whatever the reasons for the belief, a horseshoe can be turned into a very effective protective or lucky charm and the symbol can be used in all kinds of magical workings.

Chapter 14

Symbols in Nature and Sacred Geometry

Mother Nature provides us with a huge number of natural symbols and sigils in her creations. The spiral, for instance, is an ancient magical symbol and appears all over nature. Think about the shell of a snail or a fern leaf curled up before it opens out.

Sacred geometry uses sacred universal patterns right in the fabric of our reality. Sacred structures such as temples and monuments often use divine proportions, magical numbers in their calculations and design and, of course, Mother Nature uses sacred patterns in her creations too.

The world of symbols and sigils is vast and veers off into head-exploding mathematics (well for me anyway) so if you are interested do some research because it is fascinating – look up sacred geometry and also cosmology if you really want to delve deep. For the purpose of the wild witch we are going to keep things straightforward.

You can find symbols and sigils in nature or create them from natural items such as twigs or pebbles. Have a look around next time you are out and about and see how many magical symbols you can see in nature or even in buildings and on walls or other structures.

Using a symbol helps you to work with a deeper level of energy and gives your magic a bit of a boost.

Some common symbols that you might find often or use in magic are:

Circles: Yep it is simple, but still very magical, and symbolises a never-ending cycle; the cycle of birth, death and rebirth, the turning of the wheel and is also used in ritual to create sacred space and to provide protection. The circle – and the sphere –

create a unity and a completeness. On the tiniest level, atoms and cells are spherical, but you also have plant seeds and quite possibly the largest of all...planets.

Pentagram: Although you probably will struggle to find this in nature, the pentagram (five pointed star) and pentacle (with the circle around it) are ancient symbols used over the centuries by many different religions and faiths, but probably most well known now by pagans to represent the five elements of earth, air, fire, water and spirit (or ether).

Awen: If you follow a druidic pathway then the Awen symbol will be familiar to you with three dots and three rays to represent inspiration, the triple aspect of deity and the triad of sunrises.

Triquetra: The triquetra is a continuous line drawn to create three interlocking leaves and is a very ancient symbol. Its original meaning has been lost, but is often now used to represent the triple goddess (maiden, mother, crone) and the levels of earth (land, sea, sky).

Triskelion: The triskelion is a triple interlocking spiral and has been found carved on many ancient sites. It is believed to represent reincarnation.

Spiral: The spiral is found carved into the rocks on a number of ancient sites and is thought to represent the sun as it passes over the sky. I always think of Mother Earth or the Goddess when I see this symbol and it can be found all over nature.

Cross: Don't dismiss the cross symbol either because it was used long before Christianity. Draw an equal-arm cross and surround it with a circle and you get the Sun Cross or Odin's Cross, which marks the seasons and the solstices or equinoxes.

The elements also have their own symbols each a variation on a triangle.

These symbols can be drawn, painted or etched onto pieces of wood, candles or pebbles to add their magic to your workings.

Air: An upright triangle with a line running horizontally across it.

Fire: An upright triangle

Water: A triangle pointing downwards

Earth: A triangle pointing downwards with a line running horizontally across it.

Journal Prompt

Make a record of any symbols you see out in nature, maybe even take a photograph or sketch the image. If you use any symbols in magical workings keep a note of when and what for and how well it worked.

Sigils

Sigils are a personal way of drawing a magical symbol and will be unique to you. Each one will be different depending on what you want to bring in.

First you need an intent and a phrase that sums up your intended outcome.

So, for instance, let's work with: *'Prosperity and abundance for me.'*

We will use the letters of the phrase to create the sigil, but we need to simplify it first by removing the letters that are duplicated. Once you have done that you end up with: *'Proseityandbucfm.'*

Now you need to grab a pen or pencil and paper and draw the letters onto the page. You can draw them one on top of another or you can space them out linking them together – be guided by your intuition and be as creative or as simple as you want.

Once you have done that your sigil is created and can be used in magical workings. Your intent is in the letters so you can bury it in the earth, burn it in the fire or wash it away in water – whatever works for you. You can also draw sigils onto leaves and pieces of bark or paint them onto pebbles.

Journal Prompt

Keep a record of any sigil you create with details of the intent and how well it worked. This will give you a reference to check back on and re-use if it worked well or re-design it next time if it wasn't so successful.

Hill Figures

Mysterious hill figures, chalk figures and animals drawn into the sides of hills are known generically as geoglyphs (a large design or motif produced on the ground using durable elements of the landscape). They are fascinating. The images include human shapes, animals – particularly horses, giants, crosses and geometric shapes. These ancient drawings can be found across the globe.

I have several in my area and they are magical places to visit, especially if you can sit in the centre of the design or walk the chalk outline. Generally, the images seem to have been created by lifting the turf to reveal the stone or chalk beneath.

Why are they there? Well most of them are so ancient we have no idea although a lot of speculation seems to lead to the reasoning that they were for religious, spiritual or ceremonial purpose (that pretty much covers everything then...).

It is worth investigating your local area to see if there are any within a reasonable distance for you to visit.

Journal Prompt

Do your research and make a note of any hill figures in your area and, if possible, visit them and record your findings.

Crossroads

There are a heap load of folk songs that tell us the devil resides at the crossroads, but we don't really need to worry about him...

what we are more interested in is the belief that the crossing of two roads is a powerful spot. The crossroads is the centre of the four winds and the four directions. The centre point links the two worlds, that of the living and the dead – it is an 'in between' place. Although a crossroads can also be a meeting of three pathways rather than four.

In some traditions you would go to the crossroads at midnight to meet Eshu/Elegba and in others it is the place sacred to the sun god Ra and the gods Bhairava, Hermes and Mercury and the goddess Hecate. The crossroads is also a place where Hoodoo tricks take place and where spells can be buried to 'do their thing'. You may find in your local woods or even parks that there is a place where two dirt tracks cross or perhaps where a bridge goes directly over a straight run of a river or stream. That centre spot is an excellent place to work magic. It is also a good spot to dispose of magic tricks and workings after you have finished with them, including candle stubs.

Crossroads are also used in gypsy and folk magic as a place where opportunities meet and where changes in direction happen. They are unpredictable, but also offer many choices. This is a place where multiple forces come together and anything can happen; it is a place of transformation. To stand in the centre of a crossroads you will be met with power, potential and choices.

Healing crossroads spell: For any wasting or debilitating illness, borrow flour from nine different people, bring it home and bake a cake with it. Take the cake to the crossroads, say a petition for healing and leave the cake there.

Healing crossroads spell: For healing, take bread and a libation to the crossroads, pour out the libation and place the bread on the ground. Turn in all directions, each time making a request for healing and good health. Then return home without looking back

Searching spell: Stand in the centre of a crossroads (in a quiet country place obviously, not a busy intersection) and spin around until you are dizzy and fall down (please be careful) the direction that your head is in when you land is where you should begin your search.

Unblocking: Take bread and libation to the centre of a crossroads, petition the spirits to unblock your way and remove any obstacles from your path. Leave the offerings and walk away without looking back.

Let us not forget that crossroads used to be the place where people met, where travellers sought company and where gibbets (gallows) held corpses left to hang.

Journal Prompt

Seek out crossroads in your area and visit. Record how you felt and what energy you picked up on. Visit on different days and different times to see if the energy changes. If you work any crossroads magic, keep a record and see how well it worked.

Burial Mounds

A burial mound is an artificial hill shape made from earth and stones that was built over the remains of the dead. It is also referred to as a barrow, a cairn or a tumulus. Some of the burial mounds found in Europe and the British Isles date back to the Stone Age and the early Bronze Age. East Asia has burial mounds and tombs that date back to the 3rd century BCE. India and North America also have burial mounds that date back to approximately 700 BCE.

The mounds are often conical or elliptical in shape, some are even keyhole shaped and sometimes surrounded by earthworks or even moats.

A lot of the burial mounds seem to house remains of those of a higher status, but from all different religions and cultures it seems.

Check in your local area to see if there are any ancient burial sites close to you as they are definitely worth a visit. There often won't be much more to see than a grassy hill, but you should be able to pick up on some of the energies there. These are very ancient sites. Please bear in mind that they are essentially tombs of the dead, keep your protection up and treat the sites with respect and honour those that have passed.

Journal Prompt
Research your local area and see if there are any burial mounds and visit if you can (if there is free access). Record what energies you felt.

Labyrinths
One dictionary definition of a labyrinth is: *'A complicated irregular network of passages or paths in which it is difficult to find one's way; a maze.'* This explanation sounds very dry and uninteresting, but I think they are fascinating and can be walked for very spiritual reasons. There are labyrinths across the globe and some of them are ancient.

A labyrinth can be walked as a meditative journey. You follow the path as it takes you to the centre allowing your mind to be still and your body to do the movement without thinking about it. Once in the centre you can sit and release your thoughts, desires, emotions or negative energy and then walk back out of the labyrinth with a more positive outlook.

Entering the labyrinth is symbolic of the desire to cleanse, release and let go. The centre is the Divine, it is the sweet spot where you find yourself or connect with a higher power (or both). The journey back out is the new refreshed you taking the positive energy with you. You can choose to walk the labyrinth on your own or you can share the journey with others.

I once saw a young lady dance her way around a labyrinth doing cartwheels and complicated gymnastic moves...I have not tried this due to fear of injury...but the choice is yours as to how you move yourself around the pathway.

You may find there is a labyrinth in your area or there might be a maze locally. If you don't have one, then they are fairly straightforward to make on an open space of ground. You can draw out the labyrinth pathway on a large sheet of fabric or you can mark it out with pebbles, tea lights or natural items such as sticks and leaves (not on a windy day obviously).

It is a nice activity to get a group involved in from the creation of the labyrinth to walking it together.

Journal Prompt

Visit a local labyrinth or maze if there is one nearby and walk it, then record your experience. Create your own labyrinth and note how you made it and what with and your experience when you walked it.

Pathways and Ley Lines

Every road leads to somewhere. Pathways to me signify new beginnings, new journeys and finding the right direction.

Pathways are useful to work with a 'walking meditation', each step taking you deeper into the meditation to gain clarity and insight, especially if you are looking for 'some direction' about a decision or situation. Please only do this when you are in a safe spot in a large field or woodland area and not on the pavement beside a busy road.

Ley lines, dragon lines, spirit lines or song paths – all different names for the same thing. They describe straight and often geometric lines that run across the land, frequently connecting natural or sacred ancient structures or features such as long barrows, henges, standing stones, water markers, hill forts and churches. These lines are invisible to the eye, but are essentially energy pathways and they can be found across the world.

Certain landscapes really lend themselves to magic anyway

and it is worth checking your local history to find out where ley lines run in your area as these are powerful places to work from. Try Google searches or your local library for more information.

There are many places across the world that are believed to be 'Otherworldly paths'. Whether people believe the tracks were once used for religious processions, rites or celebrations or even if they are just ancient footpaths, they will all have their own individual energy signatures.

Some places are thought to be bad luck and carry the reputation of being a 'contrary place'. These were particularly believed to be places where Faerie processions travelled. Coffin paths or roadways on which the dead were carried to church are often considered unlucky too (for obvious reasons).

There is also the suggestion that ley lines are connected to astronomical points as well, some of the lines matching the path of the sun on certain festival dates for instance. Geometry has also been thrown into the mix with the idea that megalithic building crews not only worked with astronomy, but also geometry, when placing their structures.

In Australia, the aborigines believe that the creative gods walked the country, reshaping the land along pathways called 'turingas' and at certain points in the year these pathways have energy flowing through them to bring fertility and rebirth to the land. They also believe that the lines carry messages.

The Incas worked with sacred pathways that they called 'ceques'. Along these spirit lines the 'wak'as' (powerful statues or objects) were placed, which were revered by the local people.

I think, personally, it has to be how you feel about a place. Have a look at local maps and seek out the ley lines and also take note of old folk names for places because a lot of them will have been derived from the Fae or events that happened in the past and these will carry strong energies.

Journal Prompt

Find out where the ley lines are in your area and visit some of the spots, especially where they cross. Record what energy you felt.

Pathway Meditation

Make yourself comfortable. Allow the worries and stresses of the day to float away. Close your eyes.

Focus on your breathing...deep breaths in...deep breaths out.

As your world around you dissipates you find yourself in the middle of a dirt track crossroads.

The ground beneath your feet is dry and dusty. The sky above you is grey and cloudy, but the weather is warm and comfortable.

The pathway stretching out in front of you is the same dry dusty pathway that you are standing on and it appears to lead to a formation of rocks. You can just make out a gap between them where the pathway seems to continue through.

Turning to your right, the second pathway is green grass scattered with wild flowers and looks as if it stretches out to the edge of a large cornfield.

Turning again the pathway behind you is made from old red bricks laid in a complicated pattern and heads off into the distance and what looks to be a small village or settlement with lots of houses.

Then the last pathway is rich, dark soil covered in leaves. As it meanders away and on the horizon, it seems to take you to a large forest with huge tall trees and lush green vegetation.

What pathway will you take? Turn slowly and consider each option. Which pathway entices you more? Will you take the pathway that you find the most pleasing or will you take the one that worries you the most?

Make your decision.

Head off in the direction that you have chosen and see what awaits you; take your time.

When you have reached your destination spend some time there, but when you are finished head back to the centre of the crossroads. Remember you can always come back to the centre at any time and you can always choose a different pathway.

When you are ready, slowly open your eyes and come back to this reality. Wriggle your fingers and toes.

Journal Prompt

Work with the meditation and write down what thoughts, feelings or messages that you experienced.

Chapter 15

In the City

I live on the edge of a large city and I love it... I have lived in a little cottage in the middle of a field miles from anywhere and I loved that too, but I was a lot younger then and perhaps didn't appreciate the landscape quite as much as I should have done...a house in the middle of nowhere was just a brilliant place to have a party because there were no neighbours to complain.

Now I wouldn't want to live anywhere other than the city because basically I like my creature comforts (central heating, mains gas and electric, takeaways that deliver, that kind of thing). You can call me lazy if you like, but it suits me. My connection to nature is my garden, which isn't large, but is big enough to fit in my herbs and plants.

But every city still has its own unique connection to nature. Most cities will have the odd park or public garden and even city centres often have a few trees. Most urban streets have hedgerows or trees too. It is just a case of seeking them out. If you live in a city you might have to explore to find what you need, but I am pretty sure there will be something.

A city witch just needs to adapt to his or her surroundings. It is sometimes a bit more challenging to find Mother Nature at her best in the city rather than in the country, but it can be done.

Even the weeds that grow in the cracks of the pavement or walls of buildings are part of Mother Nature's tapestry and all of them can be a source of natural energy and magic.

Weeds

You will find weeds everywhere not just in the garden...but especially if you live in a city it is useful to know your weeds and recognise them because they can be used in all sorts of magic. A weed is classified as *'a wild plant growing where it is not wanted'*, so it covers all manner of different plants. In cities and towns weeds can be found growing through cracks in the pavement and between bricks in walls. Keep an eye out because I think you might be surprised at what you find. The ones you are probably familiar with are dandelions, chickweed, clover, nettles and daisies and all of these have magical uses. You may even find others such as yarrow or dock and many more, even the humble clump of grass has magical properties and energy that can be tapped into.

Chickweed (Starwort) (*Stellaria media*)

Chickweed has a strong feminine energy and is associated with the moon so it brings heap loads of emotional stuff and the power of love. At night the lower leaves of the chickweed plant fold up to protect the younger shoots, so it makes a good plant to use in protection spells for children.

Carry a sprig of chickweed with you or use one in pouches and poppets to attract love to you or, if you are in a relationship, to keep the fidelity strong.

Add a handful of chickweed in a piece of muslin to your bathwater before you go on a date to increase the chances of a love connection.

Sailors used chickweed vinegar to prevent scurvy when fresh citrus was not available because obviously when you are out at sea fruit trees are not often found...

Chickweed derived its English name from the idea that birds liked to eat it, I wonder if they know?

The Latin name *Stellaria media* refers to the little white star-shaped flowers that cover the plant.

Chickweed has a long history spanning the globe, all suggesting the use of it as a tonic to cure all sorts of ailments, not only used for people but also in the late 1500s it was a favoured tonic given to caged birds.

Clover (*Trifolium spp*)

We all know that four-leaf clovers are lucky right? Clover is said to protect the virtuous against evil forces...but only the virtuous apparently...

Clover flowers can also be carried with you to bring luck and success your way. White clover is useful in hex-breaking spell work. Red clover works well for money, luck, love and exorcism workings.

An old poem from 1815 (Sir Walter Scott) states: 'Trefoil, vervain, St John's wort, dill, hinder witches of their will.' (Trefoil being clover).

We all know that four-leaf clovers are lucky. The three leaves are believed to represent faith, hope and charity (love) and the fourth was God's grace.

Saint Patrick is said to have used a three-leaf clover to represent the Holy Trinity, the stem united three people in one God and the leaves represented the Father, Son and Holy Spirit.

Stories tell that druids would carry a three-leaf clover with them using it to help see evil spirits coming and four-leaf clovers were used for protection and to ward against bad luck.

Daisy *(Bellis perennis)*

These happy little white flowers always remind me of childhood and making daisy chains, they are such a fun cheerful flower.

Hang daisies in children's bedrooms in a pouch (safely out of the way of tiny hands) to bring protection. Have daisies in the house to make sure your home is filled with happiness, peace and joy. Put dried daisy flowers under your pillow to bring about interesting dreams.

Because the daisy flower opens in the day light and loves to show its face to the sun, it is full of solar energy, which can be harnessed and used in strength and courage spell work.

The daisy is a sacred flower of the Virgin Mary, symbolising her chastity, grace and purity.

The daisy is a symbol of love, sensuality and fertility associated with the Norse goddess Freya who also carries the association of motherhood and childbirth.

A Roman god Vertumnus became infatuated, even obsessed, with a beautiful nymph called Belides (bring out the restraining order). Belides, however, was not impressed and became so totally fed up with him pestering her all the time that she transformed him into a field of daisies…could have been worse…

The pretty little daisy is believed to have its origins in the Old English term 'day's eye' because the flower would open its petals at the start of each day and then close them at dusk and, of course, the daisy first appears each year in spring.

Dandelion (*Taraxacum officinale*)

Possibly one of the most well known and easily sourced weeds is the dandelion and it has a whole host of magical uses.

Dandelion leaves can be used in workings for healing, purification, dispelling negative energy, spirit work and weather magic. Dandelion roots can be used for divination, wishes and spirit work along with adding to dream pillows for sleep protection. Drink dandelion tea or coffee to help your psychic powers. And, of course, dandelion seeds are perfect for any kind of wish magic.

Dandelion is associated with the underworld and communication with the dead. It is an excellent herb to use for hedge riding and walking between the worlds.

Take a dandelion seed head and blow four times – once to each direction (north, east, south, west)…making a wish as you do so.

Make a wishing jar by filling an empty (and clean) jar with dandelion seeds.

The name of the genus, *Taraxacum*, has its origins in the Greek 'taraxos' meaning disorder and 'akos' meaning remedy, which reflects the medicinal qualities of dandelion. We have all blown the seeds from a dandelion globe and this led to the idea that it could predict love. If you blow away all the seeds in one big puff then you are lucky enough to be loved with a passion. However, if some of the seeds are left stuck to the stalk then there are a few things holding the relationship back. If you are really out of favour and most of the seeds are left behind then your love life needs some serious attention.

The dandelion and its sunshiny connection, along with the healing properties it has, makes it a symbol of the Roman sun god Apollo.

Dock (*Rumex spp*)

Dock takes the 'ouch' out of a situation. It calms, soothes and eases any arguments, issues or disagreements.

Sprinkle dock seeds around your house or use them in incense blends to bring in abundance and protection.

Grow dock or sprinkle the seeds around the boundaries of your work place to help with your business success and to attract new custom.

Wear dock in an amulet to bring new love or fertility to you.

An old folk tale from Cornwall tells that wet leaves of the dock placed on a burn while invoking three angels from the east will soothe the wound.

Probably one of the most famous uses for dock is to ease stinging from a nettle, by placing a dock leaf over the area. It even has a chant to accompany it, which should be said thrice: 'Out nettle, in dock; dock shall have a new smock.' No...I have no idea what it means either...

Need something to wrap your butter in to keep it clean and protected? Look no further than dock leaves, which used to be used and were often referred to as 'butter dock'.

Nettles (*Urtica dioica*)

Nettles are very good for putting into poppets or witches' bottles to remove curses.

Make a magic powder with dried nettles and sprinkle this around your property to keep out negative energies.

Use dried nettle in amulets and medicine bags to allay fear and ward against ghosts.

Nettle is mentioned in an Anglo-Saxon charm recorded in *The Lacnunga*, a 10th century manuscript. The charm is intended to be an antidote to poison and to heal infection. It contains both Pagan and Christian elements and details the Nine Sacred Herbs of Odin.

Historically nettles have held the power of protection, quite often against demons and witches...eep!

The name for this plant seems to have its origins in Anglo Saxon. The word 'noedl' or 'netel' may be a reference to the fact that this plant stings and feels as if someone has stuck you with a needle or 'noedl'. Nettle was also used as a thread before flax came along so the 'net' part of the name may also refer to 'spinning' or 'sewing'. Roughly translated 'nettle' actually means 'that with which one sews'...makes perfect sense to me.

Burning nettles while focusing on a person, a feeling or emotion will banish it (or so they say).

You can break hexes with nettles by grinding them to a powder and mixing with graveyard dirt. Burn half the mixture and waft the smoke around your body and home, carry the rest with you.

Yarrow (*Achillea millefolium*)

Carry yarrow with you to allay fears and bring you personal courage. Keep yarrow under your pillow to enhance prophetic dreams. Drink yarrow tea or burn as incense to increase your psychic powers. Bring yarrow into your home or burn it as an incense blend to invite love, happiness and peace. Scatter yarrow around your property or wear in an amulet to keep you protected.

Achilles used yarrow as a field dressing for the wounds of his soldiers during the Trojan War. He obviously didn't have enough left to use on his heel...

During the 17th century one woman was accused of being a witch because she used yarrow. At that time it was considered to be a herb of the Devil...but let's not get into the 'there is no devil in witchcraft' thing, they all had different ideas back then.

Yarrow has long been used for divination; druids used it to predict the weather and young ladies would work with it when they wanted to see who their new beau would be. In fact, in the ancient divination method of I-Ching dried yarrow heads were often used.

Journal Prompt

Take a walk around your local area and note what weeds you find, where they are growing and what the time of year is. If you collect some of the plants, document how you dried them and what magic you used them for.

Repurposing

I do a lot of re-purposing, especially with items from my kitchen; jars are a particular favourite for me. I don't like to throw things out, I recycle whatever I can and I have a lovely compost heap. But there are certain jars that I recycle for magical purpose.

Once the contents of a jar have been eaten I hold it in my hand and see what magical energy I get from it. I have found the best ones to work with are honey or pickle jars because honey is brilliant to work spells with and so is vinegar (from the pickles). I don't wash them out, I use them as they are.

Vanilla Jar Spell

I have an empty vanilla paste jar that has that witchy vibe about it because the glass is dark brown and the label is 'oldie worldy'. Vanilla carries the magical properties of love, spirituality, sex magic, passion and creativity, so it can form the base of a jar spell for any of those intents.

As vanilla is one of my favourite flavours I will use this jar for love, to keep a sense of love for my family and home. Follow your intuition...and be guided by whatever you have to hand. It shouldn't cost lots of money and you don't need to purchase lots of special ingredients. I charged the jar with my intent then added rose petals, cinnamon, jasmine, lemon balm and a couple of small pieces of sea glass (for emotions). I charged each ingredient as I put them in. When the jar was as full as I felt it needed to be, I popped the lid on and added some melted wax to seal it (okay maybe a bit did drip down the side on purpose to make it look cool...). Once I feel the jar has exhausted itself I might recharge it or if I think it is done then I will recycle of it.

Honey Jar Spells

This is a very traditional type of bottle spell. It is basically a jar that has a sweet liquid inside. You then add your magical ingredients, such as connections to the person if you are directing it towards a particular individual, herbs and maybe a written charm on a piece of paper. This is all topped off by dressing a candle with a corresponding essential oil and then the candle is burnt on top of the jar. You can use a honey or a syrup jar for this working. Honey is excellent to 'make life sweet' or to bring something or some people together. It also brings the magical energy of happiness, healing, love, prosperity, passion and spirituality – lots to choose from.

Vinegar Jar Spells

Pickle or chutney jars work really well for any kind of protection or fire magic. Once the contents have been eaten, keep the remaining vinegar in the jar and add extra items to it.

Shaking Bottle Spells

Shaking a bottle spell once you have set the magic gives it a bit of a stir up, gets the energy within the spell working and adds extra oomph. If you keep the bottle spell for an ongoing working you can regularly shake it to keep it alive.

Anything You Want...

Be creative, even an empty tomato sauce bottle would work as tomato brings love, passion, protection and creativity.

Don't stop with jars or bottles...what about tins? Once you have emptied the contents into your recipe you could use the tin for magical workings (not quite so easy to seal though).

Journal Prompt

Document any jar spells that you create, when you made them, what you used and how well they worked.

Inner City Crossroads

Every town will have a crossroads somewhere. Unfortunately not all of them will be easily accessible to bury magical items at – please don't get run over trying to dig a hole in the middle of a city running in between the traffic lights... However, if you can find a quieter road that has a crossroads it can be very useful for magical work.

If you don't have a suitable crossroads nearby you can create your own. Take some soil, salt or ground herbs and make a cross on the floor or table. The point where your two lines cross is the 'sweet spot' and you can work and lay your magic right there.

Crossroads divination: apparently, an old Persian system of divination involves standing around at a crossroads on a Wednesday (perhaps because Wednesday is linked to communication) and listen to the conversation of all the passersby. Listen to what may be seemingly random words and parts of their chat then try to apply the words to your own situation or query.

The Crossroads Keys

Another trick is to create your own set of crossroads keys. It works something like a talisman that links you directly to a crossroads so you always have that connection whenever you need it. You will need two old keys, preferably the straight skeleton kind as the modern front door keys don't work so well. Measure a piece of red ribbon or wool from your heart to the outstretched wrist of your left hand, tie the keys together with this and then carry them with you for one full cycle of the moon. Make sure you take the keys out and handle them every day; you can even tie pieces of your hair to them or add your saliva (ewww gross...but it works) so that you get a really personal connection with them.

Once the moon cycle is up you take a trip to the crossroads, dig a small hole in the ground at the centre of the crossroads and, after cutting the ties on the two keys, drop one of them into the hole. Keep the other key in your left hand and use your right hand to bury the key in the hole. You now have a key to the crossroads to use as a direct connection to open the doorway between the worlds whenever you need it.

Journal Prompt

Create your own crossroads keys and document what you used and how well it worked.

Cemeteries, Graveyards and Churches

We probably all use the words graveyard and cemetery as interchangeable, but they are slightly different. A graveyard is an older term and usually refers to a burial ground that sits beside a church. People were buried close to the church or, if they were rich enough, in crypts beneath the church.

However, as the population grew new cemeteries would be

built specifically as burial sites, but with no adjoining church. Either way they are usually very interesting places to visit, especially the older ones as they often have really fascinating gravestones.

I find them very peaceful and sacred places to be, but they are both understandably considered to be thresholds between the land of the living and the realm of the dead. Some of the older spells for protection, banishing, love and hexes call for the spell remnants to be buried in a graveyard. If you are planning on burying bits and bobs in a graveyard I would be extremely careful about doing so; you don't want to disturb anyone living or dead, you don't want to be disrespectful and you definitely don't want to get caught.

Graveyards and cemeteries, unsurprisingly, will be full of spirits, ghosts and spiritual entities – not all of them with honourable intentions, so tread carefully. Although they are places of immense power they can be used for good or bad intentions. If you are going to perform workings in such a place I would highly recommend really getting to know it very well first. Spend a lot of time there surveying the lay of the land and getting to know the inhabitants. By that I mean the animals such as squirrels and crows that you often find there, but also those souls that are buried beneath the soil.

A cemetery or graveyard is a threshold, but they usually have gates that become the 'threshold to the threshold' and the gates are often made of iron, for good reason. Iron is protective and makes an attempt at keeping out (or in) any malevolent or unwanted spirits.

The gateway of the cemetery or graveyard is also a huge place of power and is perhaps a more suitable and easily accessible place to leave any spells to 'do their thing' rather than attempting to bury them inside.

And, of course, if you find a graveyard then you will have discovered a church too. The ones with graveyards will probably be older and incredibly interesting to investigate. Often churches were built on top of pagan places of worship.

Even the newer churches have a special kind of energy about them and are worth a visit. I promise you won't turn into dust as you walk through the doors...well probably not.

Journal Prompt

Visit local cemeteries and graveyards and keep a record of when and where you visited and what energy you connected with.

Graveyard Dirt

Graveyard dirt is exactly what it sounds like...it is dirt taken from a grave. Because of the source – and by source, I mean dirt taken from the grave of a dead person – it has a habit of being used in hexes and curses. Does that make graveyard dirt dark magic? I think it depends on which grave the dirt came from and who is wielding the spell. It will also depend on what your own beliefs are about dealing with or connecting with the dead. There is no doubt either way that graveyard dirt carries a huge amount of magical power.

Personally, I love the peace and tranquillity that most graveyards have and I like wandering around investigating. I have no qualms about collecting and using graveyard dirt although these days you do have to be careful that no one sees you collecting it because being arrested for desecrating a grave is not high on my agenda. But...and here is the important part for me, you must know a bit about who resides in the grave you collect the dirt from. Dirt from the grave of a thief or a murderer is going to be fairly toxic, dirt from a doctor or physician is going to have healing properties, dirt from the grave of a soldier or service person is going to carry warrior energy – be careful who you choose.

You can if you wish just scoop up a handful of dirt from within the cemetery or graveyard boundaries, not necessarily from a specific grave, or even collect dirt and dust from gravestones rather than digging in an actual grave. This is a personal choice, you must do what works for you.

Some traditions suggest that 'real' graveyard dirt must be taken from just above the actual coffin and some practitioners state that three scoops must be collected; one from over the head, one from over the heart and one from below the feet of the body. Personally, I am not going to go to those lengths because that would definitely get me a night in the cells.

If all you need is a handful of graveyard dirt then you can just scoop it up and carefully pop it in a bag. If you need more you could take a pot plant to the grave and take home the earth that you dig out to put the plant in. I would suggest that you only do this on a relative or friend's grave – to avoid upsetting other people.

I like to get to know the spirit within the grave first, make a connection and ask permission and I also like to leave an offering. I think it is only good manners because basically you are disturbing their peace. Coins or libations are traditional gifts in exchange for graveyard dirt.

So, what is graveyard dirt used for other than hexing? Well, it actually has very strong protection properties.

Protection dirt: To protect your child as they leave your home pop a small amount of graveyard dirt on the back of your left hand then, as the child turns to go out the door, throw the dirt over their head to bring in protection.

Success spell: Using nine handfuls of graveyard dirt, mix them with salt, pepper and sulphur then burn some of it on charcoal. As it burns visualise the success and goals that you wish to achieve. Repeat as and when necessary as the power within this mixture lasts for a long time.

Journal Prompt

If you fancy collecting some graveyard dirt document where you obtained it from, what time of day, what time of year and then what you used it for and how well it worked.

Sacred Sites and Ruins

Check out your local area for any sacred sites, historic sites and buildings or ruins as they make fascinating places to visit and will often have been built on intersecting ley lines and/or hold huge amounts of ancient power.

Do investigate the energy very carefully as a lot of ruins may have been destroyed in violent attacks and you don't want to open yourself up to that kind of psychic assault.

Ruins are often good places to find interesting weeds, plants and herbs, as they seem to like growing in among the rubble and stones of decaying buildings.

Stone will also retain the energy and memories of the events and people who lived there over the duration of its useful lifetime.

Souls of those who died on the sites may also be lingering around, tied to the site in some morbid fashion.

Journal Prompt

Make a list of sacred sites and ruins that you would like to visit. Each time you do so make a note of the time of year and what energy you picked up on and record what plant and animal life was present too.

Chapter 16

Fire and Flames

Fire is a very powerful element; well, all the elements are really in their own special ways. Fire has the ability to cleanse and clear away through the force of destruction. Sometimes we do need to burn away negative influences and energy to be able to restart. Not literally of course, I am not encouraging anyone to burn down houses.

Fire can be used in spell work to burn petitions, to scry, for burning herbs and of course to provide heat for night-time rituals. *Please...* (I know I don't really have to say this but...) if you are in the woods or forest area check that you are allowed to start a fire (a lot of places don't give permission for obvious reasons). If you are given the go-ahead make sure you take the proper precautions and don't let it get out of hand. A fire in the woods or grassy fields can cause a huge amount of damage, not only to the land and plants, but also to the animals that live there.

Scrying with flames is great fun. You don't have to use a bonfire/campfire/fireplace, you can just use a candle, but you get brilliant images with a full 'set' of flames. Be mindful that fire is a fickle thing and it does like to play games with your mind though. You don't need anything special to scry with flames other than...flames...once the fire is going nicely sit back and relax, ground yourself and then gaze into the flames. Watch for any symbols that you might see, not just in the flames, but also in the glowing embers and the smoke. Also listen carefully because sometimes the fire may speak to you. You might get very clear images or even hear words, but equally you may just get flashes of images, symbols or sounds that you will need to translate. If you have some herbs to hand you can throw them onto the fire to get some interesting shapes and smoke in particular. Try using the more woody herbs as they burn for longer.

If you have a back garden you can use a fire pit or chimenea very successfully for fire magic. However, if your space is limited you can work with a cast iron cauldron or a fire-proof dish.

Simple workings can be done by using small slips of paper. If you want to get rid of a bad habit then write it down on a piece of paper and throw that into the fire. You might also like to create a chant to go with it or add in some corresponding herbs. Similarly if you are having a run of bad luck you can write that down on the paper and burn it. Gossip can be stopped by writing the rumours on paper and throwing it into the flames.

Fire magical properties: Speed, energy, passion, creativity, destruction, rebirth, purification, cleansing, sexuality, force, motion, protection, strength, authority, banishing, anger, desire, work and action.
Gender: Masculine.
Direction: South.
Elementals: Salamanders, genies.
Uses: Burning (obviously), despatching, cutting ties, purification and petitions.

Fire Meditation
Make yourself comfortable.

Allow the worries and stresses of the day to fade away. Close your eyes and focus on your breathing, deep breaths in…deep breaths out.

As your world around you dissipates you find yourself in among a grove of birch trees. The sky is an inky black smattered with twinkling stars and the crescent of a waxing moon is showing.

The air is warm around you, but you smell smoke and see a column of it rising above the trees ahead of you, so you make your way towards it.

As you step through the trees you find yourself in a wide open space in the middle of clearing. In the centre there is a large fire and people are sitting around the edge occasionally throwing what looks like bunches of herbs into the flames.

Someone is drumming and the rhythmic beat fills your body and your mind.

The folk seem friendly and you are beckoned to come and join them, so you head towards the fire and sit yourself down.

The flames are warm on your face and hands and the smell of wood and herb smoke fills your nose.

You sit quietly listening to the drum beat and allowing it to take you over.

Gazing silently into the flames you watch them dance and play seemingly to the beat of the drum.

Images appear within the flames, the sparks and the burning wood...what do you see?

The crackling of the fire holds messages just for you...what do you hear?

The flames jump and leap high and feel as if they are cleansing and purifying you completely. Allowing you to ditch any negative feelings, thoughts or emotions you had, burning them up within the fire. Setting you free.

Suddenly the drum beat slows and then stops.

You look around and realise that most of the people have already departed and the fire has died down to just glowing embers.

Thank those remaining for allowing you to be a part of it and turn and head back out of the clearing.

Slowly and gently come back to this reality, open your eyes and wriggle your fingers and toes.

Journal Prompt

Work with the meditation and write down any thoughts, feelings or messages that came to you.

There is No Fire Without Smoke

And of course, with fire and flames you get smoke, which is excellent to use not only for divination by reading the shapes and symbols you see in the smoke, but also for cleansing and purifying.

If your fire is small enough and it is safe to do, jumping over the flames works well to cleanse your entire body with the smoke and land the other side refreshed, purified and renewed.

The other option is to make smudge sticks from bundles of dried herbs. In doing this you also add the magical properties from the herbs that you burn.

Smudge Sticks

These are really simple and easy to make – literally just dry bundles of herbs and then bind them together with twine, cotton thread or wool. You can use most herbs although the woody stemmed ones tend to burn better, you can even add in dried flowers such as rose petals and lavender.

Once your smudge stick is made, light one end and direct the smoke where it is needed. You can smudge people, pets, magical tools, crystals, other herbs, rooms in your home and outside spaces.

When you have finished, remember to put the smudge stick out properly as they tend to smoulder on for a bit. I dip mine in water and then leave it to dry.

The same effect can be obtained by using loose incense, especially if you add a resin because that produces a lot of smoke. But if your preference is for incense sticks or cones then absolutely use them instead. It is the smoke produced that does the cleansing and purifying work.

Note: If you are smudging with smoke indoors please make sure to open the windows so that you don't suffocate from smoke inhalation...

Journal Prompt

Make a note of what herbs and plants you used when making smudge sticks, how long they took to dry and how well they worked.

Despacho

There is a beautiful ancient ceremony used by shamans that involves creating a despacho (not to be confused with gazpacho, which is cold soup...).

It is something like a big magic pouch that you burn or bury in the soil. The purpose of the despacho is as varied as you want it to be; it can be to give thanks for something that has happened or just life in general, but it could be for healing, a new job or general prosperity. The despacho is a gift to Mother Earth, the spirit world, deities or whatever form of the divine you choose to work with. It is an exchange for the energy that they give you.

It is quite a nice idea to cast a circle first and call upon the deity that you would like help from or to give thanks to, but you don't have to; go with your intuition.

You will need a sheet of paper – I tend to use brown paper as I can cut a decent size and it burns well – and a piece of natural string (something that will burn easily and not give off nasty fumes). Fold your piece of paper into nine squares to make firm crease lines, then unfold it (this helps when you come to the end and need to fold it all back up again).

Then you need your 'fillings'. Choose natural items and work with your intuition following the intent that you have chosen.

Suggested fillings:

Sugar: This makes life sweet and brings good things. You can just sprinkle a little pile in the centre of the paper or you can make a design with it, a spiral, a cross or a heart maybe.

Rice: For prosperity, abundance or fertility.

Dried beans: For stability, prosperity and grounding.

Salt: To bring in protection or cleansing.

Soil: To ground and bring in earth magic.

Flower petals and seeds: Use any that you are drawn to use, each one has its own magical properties.

Spices and herbs: Use ones that you feel correspond to your intent. (Full correspondence lists for herbs, foods and plants can be found in my books *A Kitchen Witch's World of Magical Herbs & Plants* and *A Kitchen Witch's World of Magical Foods*.)

Paper: You can also add slips of paper with words or drawings on.

Pretty much put in whatever you feel the need to, but make sure it will burn easily. As you add each ingredient to the despacho charge it with your intent by sending energy down through your hands or hold the ingredient up to your mouth and whisper your intent to it.

Once you have all your ingredients in place you can carefully fold the piece of paper up to keep all the items inside. Then when you have the bundle all nicely folded up, tie it securely with the string.

Next you throw the despacho into the fire, but don't watch it burn. Turn or walk away until it has disappeared. This allows you to detach yourself from the outcome of the magic.

If you don't have access to a fire big enough to burn your despacho in, it can be buried in the earth, the results will just take a little longer.

Journal Prompt

Keep a record of what you put in your despacho and how well the results turned out.

Chapter 17

Water

A bit obvious I know, but rivers, lakes and oceans are all made up from the element of water, which is a huge powerhouse of nature. Never underestimate the power of the ocean...

I love nothing more than retreating to the shores of the ocean to release any worries and other issues and come home refreshed and renewed.

Rain water can be collected in your garden in pots and buckets. Water collected from wells is often classed as 'sacred' and water from the ocean is obviously already imbued with salt, so it packs an extra cleansing and purifying punch of energy.

If you don't have access to a river or the ocean then collect rain water, use the tap in your kitchen or take a bath.

Asperging is a term often used in magic and basically it means sprinkling liquid (usually water or water with added herbs and oils) in order to achieve magical or spiritual cleansing. You can use water sprinkled on tools or herbs, but also to cleanse an area ready for ritual or magical workings.

It is totally an intuition thing, but I work with water for:

Magical properties: Fear, flowing, purification, healing, soothing, love, emotions, cleansing, motion, psychic abilities, intuition, dreams, friendships, compassion, sadness, rest and rebirth.
Gender: Feminine.
Direction: West.
Elementals: Undines, nymphs, merpeople, sirens.
Uses: Cleansing, washing away, bathing, diluting and purifying.

Water – The Magic

Although water in general has the same magical properties no matter what source it comes from, you can be more specific with the uses if you prefer. Here are some suggestions for magical properties depending on the body of water:

Dew: Beauty, health and sight.

Fog: Balance, creativity, partnerships and hidden secrets.

Rivers: Cleansing, protection, direction and moving forward.

Streams: Cleansing, purification, harmony and dispelling.

Lakes/ponds: Reflection, relaxation, peace, calm, contentment and inner work.

Rain: Cleansing, protection and energy.

Ocean: Manifesting, power, health, energy and purification.

Springs: Blessings, cleansing, protection, growth and abundance.

Swamps/marshes: Binding, banishing and hexing.

Wells: Wishes, healing, intuition and inspiration.

Waterfalls: Energy, power, prosperity and success.

Snow and ice: Transformation, creativity, balance and peace.

You can work all sorts of spells using fresh water or salt water to bring the power of lakes, rivers and oceans to your magic. Collect fresh river or stream water if you can, otherwise bottled water works well and if all else fails use tap water. If you want to clean up the tap water and get rid of some of the impurities and chemicals you can boil the water first. If you have been lucky enough to collect fresh sea water that works extremely well, but you can make your own salt water by adding...salt to water (yep you got it).

Rivers and oceans are perfect for washing away feelings, bad habits and spell left-overs. Tipping old herbs left from spell work into running water washes them away. You can write petitions on slips of paper and cast them into the ocean or rivers to allow the energy of water to work its magic.

If you don't have access to a natural source of running water you can substitute the tap in your kitchen to wash away spell work. If you need to get rid of something, then flushing it down the toilet works perfectly (but please make sure it is biodegradable).

Sea Cleansing

If you feel the need to really cleanse and purify and rid yourself of negative energy then you can petition the spirit of the sea to help you out. You can address the pure spirit of the ocean or pick a water deity to assist you. Visit the seashore and take six roses with you. Stand with your feet just in the water and one by one dip each rose into the seawater and then run it from your head down your body, your arms and your legs stroking downwards, then throw each rose into the sea. Once you have done this with all six roses walk deeper into the water (up to your waist works well, but if you don't feel comfortable go in as far as you can). Allow the waves to flow around your body six times asking for cleansing and renewal as you do so.

Then turn and walk out of the water.

To Consecrate, Purify or Charge an Amulet with Water Energy

Fill a bowl with water either fresh or salt depending on whether you want the power of fresh water or sea water. Hold your chosen amulet or tool above the bowl and visualise the ocean or a river (whichever you choose) swirling around the item. If the amulet or tool is water safe (i.e. it won't be damaged) then dip it into the water and say your intent out loud or even make up a chant.

Rivers, Lakes, Seas and Oceans

Rivers, lakes, ponds, seas, oceans, and any other names for large bodies of water, all have immense magical powers. Water is a necessity of life, never underestimate its power.

Rivers and streams have the ability to 'flow'; they bring movement so they are brilliant for removing or getting rid of things whether it is spell work that focuses on removing or dispelling or whether you just want the water to carry your spell away to do its thing. Please remember not to drop anything into any water system that won't safely degrade – not plastics or chemicals please.

The oceans and seas work well because of the power they have and the fact that they have built-in cleansing and purifying properties because they are salt water.

Ponds and lakes are slightly different because they don't tend to move much. They don't usually have waves and they don't flow like rivers, but they still hold the natural magic of water.

Journal Prompt

Research any water sources in your area and make a note of where they are to visit. Document each visit with details of the time of year, time of day and what energy you found there.

Water Meditation

Make yourself comfortable.

Allow the stresses and worries of the day to slip away. Close your eyes and focus on your breathing, deep breaths in...deep breaths out.

As your world around you dissipates you find yourself in the centre of a crossroads. The ground beneath your feet is lush green grass and the sky above you is bright blue with the sun shining down warmly on your skin.

The grassy trail before you changes part way down into pale yellow sand and appears to disappear away to a beach and the ocean shore. You can hear the waves crashing in the distance and the gulls flying overhead.

Turning to your left the next route appears to lead down to a river bank. You can see the grassy banks and hear the river flowing and the sound of otters as they splash and play happily.

Turning again, the footpath behind you seems to lead to a lake. You can see the tall bull rushes swaying gently in the breeze and hear the ducks quacking and watch as a magnificent swan takes off and flies directly overhead.

The last trackway looks as if it will take you down to an old brick well. You can just make out the bucket on the side and the turning handle.

Which route beckons to you? Will you head to the waves and the sand of the ocean, the fast-moving river flowing to an unknown destination, the calm and stillness of the lake or will you head to the secrets held within the wishing well? The choice is yours... make it...

Take the pathway that you have chosen and see what mysteries unfold for you...

Take your time, investigate the area, listen to the sounds, inspect all the plant life, the area and any animals you may come across. The pathway you choose holds answers and insight for you.

When you are ready, head back to the centre of the crossroads and know that you can revisit any time that you like.

Slowly and gently come back to this reality. Open your eyes and wriggle your fingers and toes.

Journal Prompt
Work with the meditation and write down any feelings, thoughts or messages that came to you.

Shells
Living near the sea I am lucky enough to be able to collect sea shells easily. I love walking along the beach and always come

back with pockets full of shells and hag stones.

So how about the magical properties of the humble sea shell?

Obviously, sea shells are associated with water. I often use a shell to represent west when I am in ritual, I also use them in water element witch bottles. The moon controls the tides of the ocean so shells are also associated with the lunar magic. Being associated with water and the moon I think the shell works perfectly in spells for emotions too.

Shells also have an association with the goddess Aphrodite, so can also be used for love spells. Use a shell as a love-drawing talisman.

In the past shells were also used in some parts of the world as currency, so they also have the association of money and prosperity. Use in money drawing medicine bags (with a silver coin and some mint or basil) or pop a small shell in your purse.

Think about what a shell is. It is a protective covering for the creature inside, making shells also good for protection. Use them in your witch bottles, or strung on a necklace for this purpose. You can also pop a shell on the collar of your dog or cat to bring protection.

Shells can also be used in divination, use in a set with pebbles, crystals and bones to cast a reading.

Shells can also have runes or symbols carved or painted on them. Particular shells also have their own individual meanings:

Abalone: General use and containment of empowered herbs and stones. It is also very good for love spells, balance and affirmations. An abalone amulet will protect against negative energy. Abalone talismans will bring creativity. Wearing an abalone shell will bring protection against negative energy, but also protection from depression, sorrow and fear. The abalone shell also brings creativity and inspiration. Abalone make good tools to use for balancing your chakras because it carries the colours of the rainbow. Abalone shells make good holders for incense.

Auger: Along with any long pointy shaped shells, due to their shape they bring a masculine energy...and can be used for fertility, strength, protection or courage.

Clam shells: Purification and love, but also friendships.

Conch: This shell is used to make a loud noise when blown so it works well for summoning spells, communication and clearing away confusion. It is also a symbol of truthful speech and strength and love.

Cockles: Love, friendship, relationships and emotions.

Cone shells: Time to take charge and lead by example with this shell, but it may also indicate a situation where you need to retreat or take cover.

Cowrie: Prosperity, money, love and fertility. If you look at a cowrie shell it looks very 'feminine' (i.e. yoni shaped). String cowrie shells onto red cord or a thread long enough to hang over your tummy for fertility and once you are pregnant to protect your unborn child. Make a necklace from charged cowrie shells to wear for general protection.

Whelks: Dramatic positive change and getting a grip on a situation. Also, useful for decision and direction spell work.

Limpets: Courage, confidence, endurance and strength.

Scallops: A good all-purpose shell, but also for travel and movement.

Oysters: Good fortune, love and passion, but also for banishing spell work.

Sand dollars (echinoids): Wisdom and knowledge.

Moon snails: Lunar magic, psychic abilities, purification and peace.

If you are collecting your own sea shells please make sure that the creature is not still inside any you take. If you do pick up one with a living creature toss it back into the water.

If you are purchasing your sea shells in a shop or from the

internet please make sure they are from sustainable and viable sources.

If you collected the shells from the sea shore then I don't think they need any preparation, they have the energy of the sea and the sun already in them. If, however, you purchased your shells from a store you might like to sit them in a bowl of salt water for a few hours, out in the sunlight if you can.

Journal Prompt

Keep a record of any shells you find, try to identify what they are and note how well they worked in any magic that you use them for.

Seaside Plants and Seaweed

There are many different varieties of plant life found on the sea shore and it will depend where in the world you live as to what plants you get. Get to know your local area if you live near the seashore and find out what plants grow there.

You probably won't find too many magical references or correspondences for seaside plants in books or on the net so you may have to be guided by your own intuition, which is what I always recommend anyway. Look at the plant, where it is growing, what it smells like, whether it flowers, what colour is it, what shape the leaves are etc. Get a feel for what the plant can offer you.

Grasses

Most sea shores will have at least some scrubby bits of grass growing in patches and others, particularly with sand dunes, will have large bushes of billowing grass – see the 'grass' section of this book for more details, but sea grass will have the added benefit of watery ocean magic too.

Seaweed

Seaweed is one of the obvious seashore plants and there are many different types. Listed below are two, but generally they will have very similar magical purpose and uses.

Bladder wrack (*Fucus vesiculosus*)

A brown coloured seaweed with little bubble air sacks.

Carry a small piece of bladder wrack with you for protection on sea voyages; obviously dry it first otherwise it would be a bit slimy.

Use it in any kind of magic that requires the energy of the sea (don't forget to leave an offering of thanks next time you visit the ocean). Bladder wrack also works well in weather magic especially when summoning up the winds.

Add dried bladder wrack to your floor wash to bring in more money, add a small piece under your doormat to bring money into the house too. Add to medicine pouches and sachet powders to help increase your psychic abilities.

Bladder wrack also works well for hexes. Hide a piece in the bathroom of your enemy and apparently it will cause uncomfortable infections.

Dulse (*Palmaria palmate*)

This is a red seaweed. Pick it during June and September. It is apparently quite tasty...but don't forget to wash off the snails and shells first.

To dry seaweed, rinse it in clean water to remove any sand (and those snails) then lay it on newspaper or muslin, preferably outside in the sunshine, until it is crisp, then it can be stored in jars.

Sprinkle dried ground dulse on your meal and that of your loved one to increase your desire for each other.

Hang a piece of dulse (dried, not still wet and soggy) over your front door to bring protection for your home.

Use dried dulse in your home to bring in harmony, love and peace.

Put some dulse in a jar and cover with whiskey. Keep the covered jar in your kitchen to attract good fortune.

Driftwood

Along a lot of sea shores you can find driftwood, although it does seem to depend on the particular shore and area.

Driftwood carries the energy of earth from the tree it once was and also the magic of the sea and the element of water so it gives a double whammy.

What you do with your pieces of driftwood depends on what shape and size they are, but you could string them into a wind chime, drill out holes in a piece to use as a tea light holder, craft some into a wand or use as a small altar. If you have enough small pieces you could also make a divination set. Or create a mixed set using shells, sea pebbles and driftwood.

When you collect any driftwood check it first for animal or plant life because it is often used as shelter by small animals and birds.

In Norse mythology, the god Odin and his brothers Vili and Ve created the first humans Ask and Embla from two pieces of driftwood, one was ash and the other elm.

Vikings apparently also had the habit of throwing pieces of wood into the sea before they landed on the shore. Where the wood ended up was the site for their main hall to be built and the piece of wood used to create a high seat inside.

Pebbles

Of course, if your beach has pebbles these have all sorts of magical uses, especially if you find any hag stones (see the stones section of this book for further information).

Sand

If the beach is sandy then you have found yourself another magical ingredient. Sand is made up from tiny particles of rock and minerals. Where your location is will affect the exact composition, but generally it is a mixture of silica in the form of quartz or calcium carbonate. Brilliant white sand might be made from limestone, coral and shells while yellow sand may be from granite. Black or dark sand is often from volcanic basalts.

Sand makes a very useful base to stand candles on to collect wax drips or keep an area safe from flame and it also does the same job in the base of a cauldron – health and safety conscious obviously.

To me sand also represents time and it can be used in magical workings for that intent. It can be added to medicine pouches and spell workings to represent water and all the associated correspondences. Candles can be rolled in sand before a spell to bring ocean magic in.

The tides bring changes and represent the ever-changing cycle of life. It is cleansing and brings growth and new pathways and opportunities.

The sand is also representative of all the elements: the earth, the ocean, the wind and the sun.

Think about the beach and sitting on your sun lounger, shades on, cocktail in one hand and book in the other; a perfect ideal for relaxation, so sand can bring that intent along with it.

Sand is excellent to use for banishing things, bad habits or people – write the name of the person or the bad habit you want to get rid of in the sand and then let the ocean waves wash it away. If you are at home, pop some sand in a dish, write the name and then pour water over it to wipe it away.

Use sand to create your circle in ritual. Of course sand already has salt built into it from the sea so you could use it in any magical way that you would use salt.

Either sitting on the sand or bringing some home with you

and putting it in a flat tray, you can use the sand as a blank canvas and draw whatever shapes you like. Use it as a meditative tool or create a spiral and follow it around with your finger for meditation.

Journal Prompt
If you are able to collect any sand, make a note of where it came from and when and then document the results from any magical workings that you use it in.

Sea Glass
Sea glass isn't found on the beach near me, but I am lucky enough to have family that live on the Jurassic Coast here in the UK where the beaches are littered with sea glass. What is it? Well, it is nature's way of recycling broken bottles and jars that find their way into the ocean. The pieces of glass are tumbled smooth by the natural motion of the waves. Apparently it takes about ten years for a piece of broken glass to become proper sea glass i.e. a small piece of smooth frosted looking glass like a pebble.

For me sea glass can be used in magic just as sea shells would. It is directly connected with the element of water and holds all the emotional properties that water brings, but as it was originally glass it also has a fiery element to it as well.

Use it in any kind of magical workings, but it can also be made into pretty talismans or jewellery.

Making Magical Water
Blessed, charged or magical water – whatever you want to call it, is super simple to make. Blessed water can be used for all sorts of things such as anointing (yourself, candles or magical tools), for consecrating and cleansing tools, adding to spell workings, ritual baths or even to drink.

Moon Water

You start with water (unsurprisingly) and it is your choice whether you use filtered, spring or tap water or collected rain water. If you are worried about using tap water and all the icky stuff that is supposed to be in it you can boil it first and allow it to cool. Then you need to put it in a container. I find that a glass jar works very well. At this point if you feel the urge you could charge and cleanse the water by holding your hand over the top and sending your intent into the water or you could waft some sage or incense over the top. Then you need to place the jar in the light of the moon. You can put it outside, but I would put a lid on the jar. However, you can also sit it indoors on a windowsill – it just needs to be able to catch the light of the moon. The full moon works well for this, but you could put water out in each phase of the moon and then you have different types for different spell workings.

Sun Water

Sun water can be made the same way, but obviously you put it in sunlight instead.

Storm Water

Storm water is an interesting one to make as well. Pop your jar of water outside or on the windowsill when there is a storm raging. It collects some powerful energy that you can then use when you need it.

Snow Water

Snow water can be made and all you need to do is scoop up some clean snow (I don't need to remind you not to use yellow snow do I?...), pop it in a jar and allow it to melt.

Ghost Water

Ghost water can be made by putting a bottle of water on a grave overnight during a full moon, then remove it before dawn. This can be used for hexing.

Rainbow Water

If you can catch some of the rain that falls while a rainbow is visible, this can then be used as blessed water in magical workings to bring the power of the rainbow.

Saining

Sain is a Scottish word and means a method of ritual cleansing and blessing. You will need a bottle of holy water collected from a local source (spring, river or stream, but rain water will work as well). Preferably collect it during the dark hours and on a waxing moon. Use the water to sprinkle in the corners of each room in your home or you can use it in ritual. Stand together in a circle; each person takes a sip of the water then sprinkles water on the person to their left and passes the water on.

Collect rain water during a full moon and use it to bathe your head and wash your hair to relieve stress and depression.

Flower Water

You can make magical water by infusing it with the power of flower blossoms, it then takes on the magical properties of the flower that you used.

It is easy to make, but I would recommend using wild flowers or ones grown in your garden because you don't know what process shop flowers have been through.

One method is to collect your flower petals and pop them in a jar, cover with boiling water and allow them to sit for a day (or overnight), then strain. Use straight away; the remainder can be kept in the fridge for a short time.

Another method is to use fresh flower petals and pour over just enough water to cover them. Simmer them gently in a pan until the petals become limp. Strain and allow to cool. Use this water within a day or two, keeping the liquid in the fridge.

Journal Prompt

Keep records for any magical water you create noting down times, places, sources etc. Make sure you label the bottles properly. Note what you used them for and how well they worked.

Rainbows

Such a beautiful and magical sight and although we can't actually pick, cut, dry or bottle rainbows, they can still be used in magic. There are even one or two rainbow deities such as the Greek goddess Iris, the Rainbow Serpent who is the creator in the Dreaming from Aboriginal beliefs and in Norse mythology Midgard (Earth) and Asgard (home of the gods) are connected by means of the Bifrost, which is a burning rainbow bridge. In some Native American traditions the rainbow is believed to be a pathway of the holy spirits and in Japanese cultures the rainbow was believed to be the bridge that their ancestors took to descend to Earth.

What makes a rainbow? It is all about reflection, refraction and dispersion of light in water droplets. When sunlight beams down it appears to be white even though it is actually made up of different colours that we don't usually see, but when that beam of light hits raindrops on the way down at a specific angle the different colours that make up the beam separate to form a rainbow. Rainbows caused by sunlight always appear in the section of the sky directly opposite the sun.

There are supposedly seven colours of the rainbow: red, orange, yellow, green, blue, indigo and violet. Apparently these colours were witnessed by Sir Isaac Newton, so who are we to argue? Seven, of course, is a magical number as well.

The colours can obviously be used with colour magic, but did you know you can also sing the rainbow? Singing the sound of each colour can also be worked into your spells:

Red: Do
Orange: Re
Yellow: Mi
Green: Fa
Blue: Sol
Indigo: La
Violet: Si/Ti

Of course if you work with chakras the colours of the rainbow are represented by the seven main chakras – with indigo being purple and violet being white.

Red: Root/base
Orange: Sacral
Yellow: Solar plexus
Green: Heart
Blue: Throat
Indigo/purple: Third eye
Violet/white: Crown

So rainbows bring the magic of water, sunlight and colour. The rainbow usually appears after the rain, so it brings hope, promise and healing. As it is a combination of water and sun energy, I think it works on an emotional level too. The rainbow also appears to be a connection between the earth and the sky or the Divine, so it works well for spirit or deity magic as well.

The rainbow has also been used as a symbol of diversity and I think that makes perfect sense. It brings together all the colours to make something beautiful, so it can also work magic for strength, resilience, co-operation, acceptance and harmony.

I think the rainbow is something that not only includes the colours we use in artistic endeavours, but as it is often painted by children it brings the magic of creativity, inspiration and lets out our inner child.

Apparently, it is known to be bad luck to point at a rainbow…

You can place magical items or tools at the end of the rainbow to charge and cleanse them – obviously it is difficult to actually find the real end of a rainbow (along with the pot of gold), but you could place your item on a windowsill or wall where it 'looks like' the rainbow is heading into it.

Take a photograph of the rainbow and use it in blessing magical workings.

Journal Prompt

If you are lucky enough to catch a rainbow in a photo, make a note of when and where it was taken as you can use the image for spell work. Keep a detailed record of any spell work, what you used and how it worked.

Puddles

Puddles can be found anywhere it has rained. It could be a muddy puddle in the middle of the woods or an oily puddle in the centre of the city, either way they provide very good mirrors to scry with. Take a moment to ground and centre yourself then unfocus your eyes and gaze across the puddle. If you have a question you can ask it, otherwise just ask what wisdom the water has for you. See what images you can find on the surface of the water. This works really well if the puddle has leaves or an oily surface as it provides a bit of movement.

Chapter 18

Working with the Weather

One of the useful aspects about working with the energy of any particular day or week is that you can figure the weather into your magical workings. If it is a beautiful warm sunny day you can work with the male energy of the sun or if there is a raging storm outside you can harness the powerful energy that it creates.

As for controlling the weather, that is a tricky subject. What gives you, me or anyone else the right to interfere with Mother Nature and the weather that she brings? I might want a sunny day for my garden party, but the local farmer may be desperate for rain to grow his crops, who takes precedence? Only you can make that decision for yourself and whether your needs outweigh others.

Brooms make excellent 'wands' for working weather magic as do umbrellas (open to bring rain, closed to keep it away).

Throw a broom up in the air to summon the winds. Burn the broom to stop the winds and bury the ashes.

Tie a holey stone to a cord and whip it around in the air to calm storms and settle strong winds.

Tie knots into a cord with the intent of working weather magic. When the weather is needed, untie the knots. You might untie one knot for a breeze or light rain, untie two knots for a strong wind or steady rain and three knots for gale force wind or torrential rain.

Sometimes the land is in desperate need of rain and you can work some magic to help it arrive. You can just literally stand outside and chant to the sky asking it to rain, and do a rain dance if you feel inspired to as well.

Or you can get a paper map and lay it out in front of you.

Sprinkle uncooked rice onto the areas that you would like it to rain upon. Ask the gods, deity, the divine or whoever you work with to bring rain to the identified areas. Be careful to request 'just enough' rain and not too much, you don't want floods… unless that is what you were aiming for of course.

The weather also has a whole library full of folklore attached to it and your local area probably has its fair share of weather lore too.

The wise women and men of our past would often tell the future depending on what the weather was doing at any one time, here are some of my favourites:

- Fog in January brings a wet spring.
- If the sun shines on 22nd January (St Vincent's Day) there shall be much wind.
- If bees get out in February the next day will be wet and windy.
- Fog in February means frosts in May.
- When March has April weather, April will have March weather.
- Thunder in March betokens a fruitful year.
- Thunder on April Fool's Day will bring good crops of corn and hay.
- A moist April means a clear June.
- A cloudy April will bring a dewy May.
- Hoar frost on 1st May means there will be a good harvest.
- If it rains on 24th June (St John's Day) there will be a wet harvest.
- If the 1st July is wet there will be more rain for a further three weeks.
- An unusually warm first week of August means the winter will be long and white.
- A fair day on 1st September means the rest of the month will be too.

- If there is a south storm on 19th September there will be a mild winter to follow.
- If 29th September (St Michael's Day) brings acorns then there will be snow at Christmas.
- Heavy rain in October means a very windy December.
- Fog in October means snow in the winter.
- If the October full moon is frost free then there will be no frost until the full moon in November.
- A heavy snow in November will last until April.
- If November has thunder then there will be a fertile year to come.
- If Christmas is green then Easter will be white.
- Heavy rain during the twelve days of Christmas heralds a wet year ahead.

Weather Predicting

If you want to have a go at predicting the weather yourself then it is mostly just a case of being observant and watching and seeing what happens.

If the sky is filled with thin wispy clouds very high up then you can expect good weather ahead.

Smaller puffy clouds (cumulus) seen in the morning or early afternoon with rounded tops and flat bases means there is a chance of thunder.

Big white clouds shaped like castles in the sky can indicate a lot of drastic weather happening inside.

If the clouds start to swell and become a greyish colour they will probably be thunderstorms about to happen.

A red sky at sunset means that the air is dry and dusty so the weather will be good. A red sky at sunrise means the air is clearing for a storm to move in. A clear night sky with no cloud cover and a drop in temperature means that frost could form and the morning will be a bit nippy.

A ring around the moon is a bit of a warning indicating a

warm front is coming, which means precipitation. The ring is caused by high thin clouds getting thicker as they pass over the moon, ice crystals are reflected by the moonlight causing the halo.

Animals and the Weather

Animals predicting the weather feature in a lot of folklore such as:

- When dogs eat grass, cats purr and wash, sheep turn into the wind, cows sniff the air or pigs are restless, then rain is on the way. Presumably you don't need to see all of those animals to confirm it...
- If a bull leads the cows to pasture expect rain, but if the cows head on first then the weather will be uncertain (or he is just a very gentlemanly bull).
- A cat sneezing is said to forecast rain.
- If the pigs start gathering leaves and straw then you can expect a cold winter.
- If sheep head up to the top of the hills and separate then you can expect the weather to be good.
- Wolves apparently howl more before a storm.
- When cows lie down it indicates rain.
- Horses and cows stretching their necks out and sniffing the air is said to foretell rain.
- Bats flying around late in the evening indicates good weather will follow.

Birds and the Weather

The flight and behaviour of our feathered friends can not only be used for telling the future, but also to predict the weather. Generally if the birds are flying high up in the sky then the weather is fair, but if they detect a storm coming they will take refuge on land. They also fly much lower if the air pressure is falling. Birds will also tend to become silent before a storm too. Here is some folklore:

- Hawks flying high means a clear sky. When they fly low, prepare for a blow.
- When fowl roosts in daytime, expect rain.
- Birds singing in the rain indicates good weather is on the way.
- A single crow flying alone is a sign of bad weather, two flying together signals fine weather.
- A rooster that crows before bed indicates he will rise to wet weather.
- When a swallow builds the nest high, the summer will be dry; when the swallow builds low, you can safely reap and sow.

Journal Prompt

Keep a weather journal making notes each day of the temperature and weather conditions and how it makes you feel and affects your emotions. Also, make a note of any birds or animals and see if you can predict the weather.

Snow and Ice

Where I live, we don't tend to get a lot of snow and if we do it isn't usually very much and it doesn't stay long. However, if you do have snow then you can make all kinds of magic with it.

Basically, snow and ice are variations on frozen water so it carries all the magical properties that water does, such as healing, cleansing and purifying, and it is a very feminine energy. But because snow and ice are water in a transformed state they also bring the energy of transformation.

When you collect your snow will also change the energy. For instance, if you scoop up a handful of the white stuff when fresh snow has laid and the land is still and silent it can be used in spell work for calming tempers or soothing situations. If you collect snow during a raging blizzard then it will pack a huge powerful punch of energy.

If you are tempted out into the snow, once you have finished your snowball fight, what about that snowman? Think about it...a figure shaped from snow, does it remind you of anything? How about a large snow poppet? Build him by your front gate and charge him with protection duty.

If you want to get rid of a bad habit or feeling or even a person, the general idea is to write their name or the thing you want to banish on a slip of paper and pop it in the freezer. But you can work this spell using snow instead by burying the piece of paper or even writing the name or word in the snow. As the snow melts it takes away the item with it.

You can also write your wishes and goals in the snow; as it melts your intent is released to the universe.

Another way to get rid of bad habits or emotions is to dump those feelings into a snowball and throw it away from you as far as you can.

If the snow outside is quiet and peaceful, to make the most of that perfect stillness get wrapped up warm and go and sit outside for a bit. Allow your mind to clear and see what messages the divine has for you.

Collect a jar full of snow and once it has melted use it as 'snow water'. The same can be done with ice or icicles; pop them in a jar to melt.

Basically, both ice and snow will eventually melt and in doing so they can take negative energy with them as they do so, cleansing and purifying as they go.

And of course...we mustn't forget lying down on the ground to make snow angels...

Journal Prompt

Keep a record of any magical workings using the snow or ice

you collected, what else you used and how it turned out.

Storms

Storms bring with them a huge powerful punch of energy, so if there is a storm raging above you take advantage of all that magic. Torrential rain, thunder and lightning can be directed into all sorts of spell work. Work your spell with the storm overhead and visualise the energy from nature being directed down into whatever your magical working is. If you are feeling brave you can even stand outside in the storm and channel that energy through you; if you prefer to stay warm and dry then do your magical working by a window where you can see the storm. Obviously it goes without saying that to stand on top of a hill in a lightning storm is not advisable.

Storm Water Cleansing

Collect rainwater during a storm then add this to your bathwater and also rinse your hair in it. Ask for cleansing and renewal as you bathe. The same can be achieved by collecting rainwater during a storm then heating the water up in a cauldron and wafting the steam over your body. Be careful not to scald yourself though.

Rain

As I sit writing today it is raining. I like to sit in our conservatory so I can see our garden clearly and hear the rain as it hits the roof. I find it a very soothing and hypnotic sound.

I am also just back from the short walk for the school run. Everyone is hurrying along hidden beneath their coats and umbrellas, but I like to take my time and feel the rain as it falls. It is after all water and that brings with it the magic of cleansing and purification. Rain is also linked to emotions, so if you can connect with it and allow the water to literally wash over you it can help bring clarity and relief. For me the absolute best place to really experience rain is to be on the sea front with the ocean in front of me and the rain falling from above me; such power from the elements.

The first spring rain is thought to be especially magical. Place a container outside at the spring equinox to collect the first rain. Use this rainwater to bathe in for a whole year of luck and happiness. Wash your face in it to bring youth and beauty. Wash your hair in it to keep romance alive. Sprinkle the water around your home for good luck and abundance.

Chapter 19

Wind and Air, Moon and Sun

The power of the wind is mighty and can be used for all sorts of spell work because not only is the wind refreshing, cleansing, purifying and full of the energy to aid with clearing out all kinds of unwanted baggage, it can also be used differently depending on what direction the wind is coming from.

Invoking the winds for magical purpose is an ancient art and there are plenty of deities associated with the winds.

One of the main uses of wind in magic is to bring about change, especially when using the energy from an east wind if your purpose is for new beginnings. The east wind brings renewal and can be used for any kind of spell work that involves the intellect, such as intuition and psychic abilities, but also for beginnings, improvements or transformation.

A wind from the south is hot and fiery, bringing with it the power to work curses, hexes or any negative magic, but also purification, love, lust, vitality and passion. South winds are also good for working banishing magic whether it is for toxic people, jealousy or selfish actions.

West winds swing in with fertility and love and to help with healing, cleansing, strength, emotions, happiness, sleep and dream work.

The power of the north wind is one of sudden and unexpected changes that may require a bit of attention and work to deal with. However, the north wind also helps dispel bad habits and can be used for material gain, money, prosperity and organisational skills.

Air in general is a courier of messages and our breath itself can be used as magic to breathe energy and intent into items, to whisper petitions to the wind and to cleanse and purify objects.

To turn things on their head, the wind can also be used very successfully for curses. Stab a knife into the wind and wrap it carefully in a piece of fabric. The knife can then be used to send a hex into whatever spell you stab it into to (a poppet for instance) with the full power of the wind behind it.

Wind/air magical properties: Movement, intelligence, divination, concentration, visualisation, travel, study, freedom, knowledge, lost items, thought, teaching, happiness, beginnings and communication.
Gender: Masculine.
Direction: East.
Elementals: Sylphs, winged faeries.
Uses: Throwing items to the wind, fanning, visualisation and cleansing/clearing.

Moonlight

The moon is a key part of witchcraft and working with her phases can add structure, purpose and focus to your life and an extra oomph of power to your spells. The simplest moon magic spell of all is to just stand outside under the moon, hold your arms open wide and look up...talk to her...

It is a huge subject, so I won't go into detail (blatant book plug alert...see my book *Pagan Portals –Moon Magic* for more information) but here are the moon phases and their magical correspondences:

New moon: A good time to work magic for letting go of all those negative energies and bad habits and also to start work on new projects (once you release something negative it is advisable to fill the void with positive stuff). Be creative, plan, plot and scheme, apply for a new job, house hunt, bring about changes, good luck and growth.
Waxing moon: Good for animals, business, change, emotions,

matriarchal strength. Represents the zest of life with the aid of stability. Helps bring forth courage and optimism. A good time to replenish and revitalise, boost your energy, but also conserve your strength as it is easy to do too much, be active, increase your communication, let go of that which isn't working and bring focus in.

Full moon: Work with divination, reflect on your goals, feelings and emotions. This phase is good for transformations, psychic abilities, strength, love, power and fertility. Cleanse, purify and charge your crystals and tools.

Waning moon: Go with the flow, have a clear out, analyse situations, feelings and projects, follow your needs and reactions, meditate, let go, release, banish, reverse, work with divination for insight.

Journal Prompt

Keep a moon diary recording each phase of the moon and how it affects your thoughts, emotions and wellbeing. Also, make a note of any magical workings, in what phase you did them and how well the results turned out.

Sunshine

I think sometimes as a witch the moon tends to get pride of place and the sun perhaps takes a back seat. But it is an incredibly powerful source of natural energy and magic.

The sun is a very strong masculine energy that balances with the feminine energy of the moon.

Sunshine rays can be used to charge tools and crystals, to cleanse and purify pretty much any object or even yourself. They can even be focused through a magnifying glass onto paper or dry leaves to create fire.

And, just like the moon, the sun has phases that can be used to tie in with your magical workings to add an extra boost of power:

Sunrise: Basically when the sun wakes up and peers over the horizon. This phase is all about new beginnings, changes, health, employment, renewal and finding the right direction. It can also be very cleansing.

The morning: This is when the sun is growing in strength, so it brings the magical power for growth, positive energy, resolutions, courage, harmony, happiness, strength, activity, building projects and plans, prosperity and expansion of ideas.

High noon: When the sun reaches its peak in the sky at midday, work magic for health, physical energy, wisdom and knowledge. It is also a good time to pop your tools or crystals out that need charging. (Note: some crystals can fade in strong sunlight so check first before putting them out).

The afternoon: The sun is heading back down and the energy now is good for working on business matters, communication, clarity, travel, exploring and anything professional.

Sunset: As the sun takes itself off down below the horizon work magic for removing depression, stress and confusion, letting go, releasing or finding out the truth of a situation.

And just as there is a tradition of drawing down the moon and her power into your body you can do the same with the sun. Stand outside on a sunny day at the time of day of your choosing. Make yourself comfortable with your arms thrown open wide. Allow the energy and warmth of the sun to enter your body, filling you with energy. Either feel the energy entering your body via your hands and running through your veins to every body part or visualise breathing in the sun energy through your mouth. When you feel that you are finished, remember to thank the sun. Note: do not stare directly into the sun as it can damage your eyes.

Journal Prompt

Keep a sun diary and record how much sunlight (or cloud cover) there is each day and how it affects your moods and emotions. Also, detail any spells you have done, what time of the day you worked with them and what the results were.

Chapter 20

Divination

Nature provides any manner of different ways to work with divination, from creating your own set of ogham staves from sticks or a rune set from discs of wood to creating a lithomancy set from stones and shells. Divination can also be found by taking notice of what is happening around you; in the clouds or flight of the birds and the like – be vigilant and track the signs that nature is offering to you.

Even something as simple as sitting watching the leaves fall from a tree can give you answers, if you ask the right questions.

Wild Witch Runes

It is really easy to make your own set of runes. I have created 'wild witch runes' using symbols from nature and assigned meanings to them that seemed right for me. You can use any images and you don't have to be an artist to draw them. Paint the images onto pebbles, shells, glass pebbles, discs of wood or modelling clay.

These are the images and meanings that I used for my set:

Flower: *Creativity, natural beauty and inspiration*
Flowers are beautiful and come in all shapes and sizes, their beauty and colours can bring inspiration and creativity in many forms. Take a look around you and see the beauty of nature and be inspired to create and shape your life in the way that you really want it to be. This may also herald a creative period in your life... you are the designer of your own destiny...shape it well.

Sun: *Success and happiness*
The sun has got his hat on...hip hip hip hooray! Sunshine brings

success, joy, happiness, fun, smiles and all the other good stuff. Either this good ju ju is on the way or you are enjoying it now. Sit back and soak up the rays and give yourself a pat on the back for creating this successful happy situation. The sun brings a joyful solution and a period of fabulousness...make the most of it.

Moon: *Intuition, veils and illusion*

Mysterious and beautiful she hangs in the dark night sky bringing intuition and illusion with her. Listen to that inner voice and trust your instincts, they will never let you down. The moon can also create illusions by drawing a veil across the truth...use your spidey senses to see through the mists and find the reality.

Water: *Emotions, cleansing and purifying*

Oh, that wet stuff sure does bring on the emotions, get out the tissues and prepare yourself. Emotions can be extremely powerful, but...if you hold them in they can cause a lot more damage than letting the flood gates open. Have a good ol' bawl...release...cleanse and let it all go. Water is purifying and cleansing and can clear out all those negative emotions you have been hanging onto.

Crossroads: *Decisions and choices*

Hmmm choices? Decisions? Sometimes they can be tricky blighters to deal with, too many choices or not enough? Some decisions are also hard to make. There are usually no right or wrong decisions only the right ones for you and that means you have to put on your big girl or boy panties and make that choice. Use your intuition, weigh the pros and cons, but ultimately make the right decision for *you*.

Wind: *Changes and transitions*

Ch...ch...changes...most people are uncomfortable with change, but the only real definite in life is that things change. Life is fluid and ever moving and you have to go where the winds of change take you. Fighting against the force will only get you caught in a tornado. Some changes can be really difficult to deal with, but often they turn out to be the best thing that ever happened to you...trust.

Acorn: *New beginnings and growth*

Great things from tiny acorns grow...really they do. Think about how tiny an acorn is and how huge an oak tree becomes. This is a sign of new beginnings, projects, journeys and a bit of personal growth thrown in for good measure and you can never have enough of that. Plot, plan and scheme and dig out those hopes and dreams you had stashed away because it is time for you to shine.

Owl: *Wisdom and learning*

Perhaps some form of new learning is coming your way from a mentor or a course. Keep an eye out for it and be open to what the universe sends your way, it may push you out of your comfort zone but run with it. Alternatively...the owl says: 'Use your brain.' You need to take a step back and see the bigger picture, draw on your intellect and use the little grey cells you were blessed with to think yourself out of the situation.

Shoot: *Fertility and abundance*

The dark brown earth is bare until the tiniest of green shoots starts pushing its way through the surface to the sunshine. Fertility and abundance are coming your way baby! No pun intended because fertility doesn't always mean the pitter patter of tiny feet (although it can), it may also mean the fertility of new ideas, new friendships, new prospects and new directions. With that fertility also comes the opportunity of abundance and prosperity.

Ivy: *Binding, partnerships, love and friendships*
Binding is such a foreboding word and it can be restrictive, but it can also be safe and secure. Ivy is all about partnerships whether it is in the va va voom, lurve thang, BFFs or grown-up business partnerships – which one feels right for you? Enjoy that feeling of belonging, being cared for and sharing, but just be a bit wary of it getting too tight for comfort; it happens sometimes.

Tree: *Grounded, strength and stability*
Tall, strong and sturdy with big ol' branches, the tree brings a sense of grounding and stability with a heap load of inner strength to carry you through. Push your feet into the soil of Mother Earth and make that connection. She will help you stand strong and firm without wavering. Tap into her solid energy and become superman or woman, just maybe without the spandex.

Snail: *Solitude and withdrawing*
Forgiving all the snails that eat the plants in my garden, this rune is all about solitude and withdrawing because we all need a bit of alone time on occasion. It is good to take a step back and hide in your woman/man cave for a bit, find yourself, balance your inner being and reflect. Take your time just remember not to stay there too long...there is a big ol' fabulous world waiting outside for you.

Web: *Fate, life coming together and weaving the web*
Spider webs are beautiful intricate creations and mirror the web of life. We weave our own webs and create our own links, connections and pathways bringing them all together with us in the centre. How are you creating your own web? Does it need a tweak here and there? *You* are the creator, *you* have the control... weave it...

Sun | Moon | Flower | Water

Crossroads | Wind | Acorn | Butterfly

Shoot | Ivy | Tree | Snail

Web | Bones | Snowflake | Owl

Bones: *Death, endings, letting go and releasing*

First of all, *don't panic!* Seriously don't...the death rune is not about a pile of bodies, but about the ending of things. Cutting the cords, letting go and releasing. Everything comes to an end at some point and of course you must have death to have rebirth. When an ending comes it just makes way for a different new beginning. Let it happen…and welcome the new start.

Snowflake: *Obstacles, issues, problems and overcoming*

There may be trouble ahead…but the universe likes to throw obstacles and problems our way as little life challenges just to see how we deal with them. And of course I am pretty sure it will keep throwing the same issues at us until we actually learn how to deal with them properly. Obstacles were made to be overcome and lessons will be learnt along the way. Buckle up buttercup and tackle it head on.

Butterfly: *Balance, harmony and equilibrium*

I suspect many of us are always looking to find the balance in all things, whether it is life, work, spirituality, family or relationships. Balance equals harmony. But it ain't always easy, that's for sure. Sometimes it can feel like you are definitely on the heavy end of the seesaw. I could say all it takes is a little adjustment to set it straight and sometimes that is the case, but occasionally it takes a bit more effort and a whole lot more shuffling around. It will be worth it, I promise.

Dowsing

The art of dowsing was traditionally a method of divining for sources of underground water, but it can have other uses. The tool used in dowsing is usually a wooden Y-shaped stick, often from the hazel tree (although copper rods or pendulums are sometimes used as well). The Y part of the stick is held – one side in each hand and the long part of the Y points forward. Sometimes two bent sticks or wires are used, one held in each hand. The sticks move when they find water or ley lines or whatever it is you are seeking.

Flower Casting

All you will need for flower casting is a selection of flower petals and leaves along with either a plain square of fabric or a bowl of water. This divination works best at night-time and preferably in the light of the moon. Focus on a question you want answered, then gather up the flower petals and leaves in your hand and scatter them either on the cloth or the surface of the water. Note what patterns or images you see, where do the petals and leaves land? Are some clumped together? What does it mean to you?

You can give more detail to this by assigning meanings to each different type of flower or leaf and designing a map on the fabric, sectioning it into quarters to represent the directions perhaps, so west would be all about emotions and north represents home life. You get the idea.

Scrying

Scrying is the art of telling the future using a reflective surface, which can be a crystal ball, a mirror or the surface of any body of water. I like to use a bowl that has a dark inside and fill it with water then I add something to help the images such as popping a silver coin in the bottom or you could scatter flower petals, leaves or herbs onto the surface. Scrying is easier to work with at night-time under the light of the moon, but it can be done in the dark with a well-positioned candle. See what images appear on the surface of the water and try to decipher what they mean to you.

Aeromancy

Divination conducted by interpreting atmospheric conditions, so basically it is weather divination.

Apantomancy

This is divination using whatever you have to hand or what items present themselves to you seemingly by chance. Apantomancy also covers the chance meeting or sighting of animals. For instance a black cat crossing your path would come under this category.

Augury

Augury is the practice of divination using natural phenomena, especially by observing the flight and behaviour of birds. You can facilitate this divination by sprinkling seeds or breadcrumbs on the ground and watching how the birds land, eat the food and the fly away. So, if they fly off to the right after eating then your answer is positive, if they fly off to the left it is negative and if they scatter randomly then the situation is either very complicated or you need more information to solve it (or a cat has just jumped in between them…it happens).

Austromancy

A form of aeromancy, this is divination by observing the winds, particularly the south wind.

Botanomancy

The burning of leaves, wood and herbs produces smoke and flames, which can be read to determine answers to questions or foretell the future. This is the art of botanomancy.

Capnomancy

Divination using smoke. It requires watching the smoke after a fire has been created. The shape and the direction of the smoke will give the answers.

Daphnomancy

A form of pyromancy that predicts the future by burning bay (laurel) leaves. The sound and amount of crackling that the burning leaves make gives the answer.

Earth Divination

You will need four people for this system and a clear patch of ground that is just dirt with no weeds or plants. Sit around the patch of earth with each one of you sitting at a point of the compass; so that would be north, east, south and west. The person sitting at the west point draws a circle in the earth with a stick. Then all four study the surface of the earth within the circle and make predictions.

Hydromancy

Throw a pebble into a pool of water and what do you get? Ripples... By watching and translating the ripples, the ebb and the flow of the water, you can get your answers.

Lithomancy

Lithomancy is a set of items that you throw and determine what they mean by where they land. I like to include shells, seed heads, small bones and sometimes crystals in my lithomancy set too.

Oracles

If you are creative or artistic you could make your own set of oracle cards; drawing or painting images of plants and flowers onto pieces of card. Pressed flowers and leaves also work well for this.

Pendulums

You can make a natural pendulum fairly easily, something like a hag stone or a shell is very simple to thread onto a piece of string and works really well for pendulum readings. You could also tie a small piece of wood to the end of a string too. This works with plant matter as well, but you have to use a light thread and a heavier plant such as a big poppy seed head or dried rose bud otherwise it doesn't hang properly.

Phyllorhodomancy

This one is all about roses...divination taken from roses, rose leaves and rose petals. You hit the rose against your hand and interpret the sound. This evolved to include a young lady picking a rose on Midsummer's Eve and wrapping it in white paper then storing it away. The first man who found the rose and removed it was the one destined to marry her. This also included how well the dried rose kept its colour. If it faded quickly then the lover was untrue. And, of course, the rose can also be used to pluck the petals while saying the old phrase: 'He/she loves me, he/she loves me not.'

Pyromancy

One of my personal favourites...this is divination by fire as in reading messages from the flames. How fierce the fire burns, what colour and shape the flames are and how things burn that you throw on to it such as sticks and herbs.

Snail Divination

You will need a willing snail for this, although how you tell whether a snail is willing or not I don't know. You will also need some ashes from the fire. If you don't have ashes then flour works as well. Put a layer of the ashes or flour on the ground and gently place a snail in the middle. Allow the snail to wander around. The divination comes from the snail trail shapes and symbols he leaves in the ashes/flour. It may take some time...

Xylomancy

Divination using twigs, pieces of wood or fallen tree branches. What shape they are, colour, thickness, position and any unusual characteristics of fallen branches and twigs that appear in your pathway. This evolved into creating sets of twigs that are thrown to form random patterns.

Journal Prompt

Detail any divination you work with; how, when and what you worked with and then the results. How well did you connect with the tools and what were the results like? You will find that some divination tools work better for you than others.

Omens and Signs

Keep an eye out for any signs and signals from nature. One of the most common and well known is finding a feather in your pathway (a sign from spirit/the angels), but there are many more. What about a poorly house plant? If you have been looking after it properly, is it a sign of a sickly relationship in the family? Take a look in the garden; are there plants growing together or entwined that don't usually mix? It could be a sign of love or a relationship. Don't forget the plants that self-seed in the garden, where are they growing and what type of plants are they?

Also, keep an eye on the TV, films, advertising and books – if you find the same plant or animal popping up then it could be a message.

Don't get hung up about it all though, sometimes a weed is just a weed and a coincidence is just that. Trust your intuition to know which are messages or have meaning and which aren't.

Here are some that I know of:

- If a bee flies into your home you will soon have a visitor (other than the bee). If you kill the bee you will have bad luck (and so you should) or the visitor will be an unpleasant one.
- A bird in the house was said to be a sign of death – but I wouldn't panic too much, death can mean the ending of something, it doesn't have to mean a dead body.
- If you say goodbye to a friend while standing on a bridge, it is said that you will never see them again.
- If the first butterfly you see in the year is white then you will

have good luck all year.

- Seeing three butterflies together is very lucky.
- And of course, the good ol' black cat. If a black cat walks towards you then it brings good fortune, but if it walks away from you it takes the good luck with it (the solution is to always have kitty treats in your pocket).
- Don't step on a crack in the pavement – I used to think the bears would get me (we don't have any bears here), but it comes from the rhyme: 'Step on a crack, break your mother's back.'
- A cricket coming into the house brings good luck with it.
- A dog howling at night when someone inside is poorly is a bad omen.
- Finding the first flower of spring has a meaning depending on what day of the week you find it: Monday is good fortune, Tuesday is success, Wednesday is marriage, Thursday is a warning to keep an eye on your money, Friday means prosperity, Saturday means bad luck and Sunday means good luck for a few weeks.
- Catch a falling leaf on the first day of autumn and you won't catch a cold all winter.
- If a white moth tries to enter your house keep it out because it is said to foretell death (an awful lot of these relate to death don't they?).
- Seeing an owl during the daytime is said to be bad luck.
- Make a wish on the first robin of spring that you see, but make sure to finish the wish before it flies away.
- If you see three seagulls flying directly above you, check your life insurance because it is a foretelling of death (yep another one).
- Killing a sparrow brings bad luck (just don't kill any birds okay?) because the sparrow is said to carry souls of the dead.
- Seeing a spider run down its web means you will be taking a trip.

Chapter 21

Animals and their Meanings

There are many different types of animals that can be found in our forests and fields – all of them can provide us with magical properties, whether it is in the form of messages, meanings or animal spirit guide energy. If you see an animal or bird when you are out and about, try to connect with the energies that it brings. If you aren't able to do so at the time make a mental note of the animal, the colours, how it runs or flies then later on sit and meditate to make a connection with that animal to see the reason it made itself known to you.

And, of course, you can work with specific animals in spell work to draw on their individual energy.

There are plenty of websites that can give you animal spirit guide/totem meanings, but here are some of the animals I have encountered and their meanings. If you connect with a particular animal you may relate to some of the 'book' meanings, but don't be restricted by them. Use your intuition and connection with the animal spirit guide to see why it has come to you and what it means to you personally.

Ant

These little blighters have a habit of building a nest in the wall of my conservatory and then swarming inside...

Probably the most noticeable thing about ants is that they are incredibly industrious. The ant is also part of a much larger community. Each ant has its own duties and they all work together in harmony to get the job done. They work hard, co-operate with each other and are patient (patience is really not one of my virtues). Ants are also great architects and create elaborate and detailed ant mounds and tunnels, they are persistent and using their skills can make dreams into reality. Ant can also help you to let go of your ego.

Ant medicine is hard work, teamwork, community, perseverance, patience and achieving goals.

Bee

This little guy in his stripy pyjamas is incredibly important to the planet. The bee works in a very social environment and as part of a team with an intricate hierarchy. He brings the value of family, good communication and the importance of home life and community. He also works extremely hard and is incredibly productive, which basically means you have to work for what you want, but if you do put the effort in you will achieve your goals. He is a little bundle of fuzzy buzzy life.

Bee medicine is love, life, order, growth, productivity, wisdom, family, community, teamwork, mystery, provision, nurturing, organisation and communication.

Blackbird

The blackbird was considered to be sacred to the gods in many cultures because of its song. The Greeks, Welsh, Irish and druid traditions believed the song of the blackbird could expand our consciousness and provide not only healing, but also allow us to uncover mysteries from our unconscious mind and dreams. The song of a blackbird helps us to find purpose and meaning in our spiritual and mundane lives.

There is a suggested connection between the blackbird and the blacksmith, the blacksmith being a master of all the elements and definitely Otherworldly. Blackbird brings that blacksmith magic in the form of creativity and inspiration; he also helps you unlock hidden potential from within.

Blackbird is also a good animal to help you with meditations, journeys and trance work. He can awaken and enhance psychic abilities, bringing healing and clarity with him. He can show you how to be determined and focused and use your abilities to your fullest potential. He teaches us to use and rely on our intuition and how to connect with all things. He asks you to listen to everything around you and to become connected, grounded and balanced.

Blackbird medicine is healing, mysteries, unconscious mind, spirituality, the Otherworld, elements, magic, creativity, inspiration, meditation, psychic abilities, clarity, focus, intuition and connection.

Butterfly

Butterfly flits in by showing us the different stages of life that we go through from uncomfortable pupa right through to beautifully painted wings. She is a perfect symbol of transformation. She asks that we accept and even embrace the changes that come our way, to go with the flow rather than fight against the tide.

Butterfly medicine is time, grace, growth, soul, elegance, expansion, surrender, transformation, expression, transition, resurrection and vulnerability.

Crow

The crow is a dark and mysterious creature, but one that is incredibly wise, intelligent and wickedly naughty. He represents mischievous behaviour, but one that can have very dangerous consequences. He has the balance of joviality and the darkness. The crow holds the wisdom and memories of the ancestors and can remind us that we need to look to the ancients for understanding, although the crow is often stubborn and wilful so you may have to dig deep to get the information that you seek.

Crow is a creature of the Otherworld and often linked with death, but is also brave and courageous.

Crow medicine is about the trickster archetype, fun, magic, curiosity, secrets, confidence, bravery, protection, arrogance, mysteries, unpredictable and the wisdom of the ancients.

Deer/Stag

Such a beautiful and graceful creature, the deer is often associated with poetry and music and the world of Faerie. Did you know that deer also have a keen sense of finding the best patches of herbs and plants to eat? Deer helps us to seek out our inner self and open up to spiritual experiences. Deer also has a huge capacity for generosity; open up and trust her to guide you and you will not be disappointed.

Deer medicine is grace, peace, love, beauty, fertility, humility, regrowth, speed, creativity, spirituality, abundance, faerie, benevolence and watchfulness.

Dragonfly

Dragonfly flies in on the breeze, bringing the element of air and changes. He asks that you listen to the changes on the wind and deal with them rather than allow them to blow up into a storm. Dragonfly is also a creature of the water so he brings our subconscious mind into the mix. Deal with those buried feelings and pay attention to your inner thoughts.

Dragonfly medicine is changes, prosperity, luck, strength, peace, harmony, purity, dealing with issues, intuition, dreams and our subconscious.

Fly

Yep even that annoying fly that flits about and won't sit still long enough for you to get rid of it...ahem...has meaning in the world of animal spirit messengers. He brings the message that quick changes are heading your way; he warns you to be prepared, but also to never give up. He brings persistence even if it is annoying or even selfish. You have the ability to reach your goals.

Fly medicine is survival, persistence, reaching goals, vision, dealing with issues, changes, transformation and adapting.

Fox

I live on the edge of a big city in a mid-terrace house with a small garden, which is enclosed on all sides by a high brick wall. To get into my back garden (other than via the back door obviously) you would need to scale several 6ft and 10ft walls and climb over a lot of sheds...

This morning I opened the back door to find a large fox sitting in the garden among a pile of flower pots... We often get foxes in the street and they do like to empty our dustbins at the front of the house, but this one must have been a particularly gymnastic creature to find its way into our back garden. Unfortunately as soon as he saw me he ran across the garden, scaled the 6ft brick wall into next door and then over their back wall (10ft high).

As foxes are generally seen at dawn and dusk; it links them to the time of 'in between' and the world of magic. Fox is clever and cunning along with being agile and skilful. He can teach us how to detach from our surrounds and use all our senses for observation and not only to anticipate what will happen, but also to shape and create our own future. He teaches us how to outwit and remove ourselves easily from unpleasant situations. He does remind us, however, that being crafty all the time can backfire.

Fox can help us with our people skills in knowing when to take a step back, when to detach or when to wade in. He helps build intuition skills. He also guides us with judgement, bringing patience and the ability to listen and sense before making a response. The power of fox teaches us to live and connect with all that is around us, to blend in with our surroundings and become a part of the all.

Fox's wisdom includes: shape-shifting, cleverness, observational skills, cunning, stealth, camouflage, feminine, courage, invisibility, the ability to observe unseen, persistence, gentleness, swiftness, wisdom, reliable friends, magic, shape shifting and invisibility.

Mouse

On occasion my house gets a small mouse invasion and boy can they move fast...

Mice like to live underground and burrow and this gives them a strong connection to the Otherworld. Some folklore suggests that mice carry the souls of the deceased. Mice are apparently incredibly clean and constantly grooming themselves, perhaps so that they look good for all the other mice because they sure are fertile. So, if mouse has appeared maybe he is indicating that you need a bit of a tidy up...

Mouse medicine is modesty, grounding, resourceful, adaptability, shyness, innocence, fertility, awareness, voracity, determination, conservation and cleanliness.

Otter

These amazing creatures spend a lot of time in the water and because of that they have a deep connection to the divine feminine, initiation and the cycles of life. Water also has the properties of healing, creativity and transition. Along with the water connection the otter also brings the magic of the moon. If you have ever watched otters at play you will also know how full of energy and agility they are too. He reminds us that all work and no play makes for a very tired, boring otter.

Otter medicine is lunar magic, water magic, happiness, agility, energy, curiosity, creativity, dexterity, protection, friendship, initiation and fun.

Robin

Although we often see images of them on Yuletide cards, seeing a robin is actually one of the first signs of spring. He brings with him new beginnings, new adventures and celebrations. His bright red breast is a symbol of the returning sun and his bright yellow beak speaks the truth. He can bring a new perspective and shed clarity on a tricky or confusing situation. His cheerful song shouts at us to get up and get going and to enjoy the life that we have been blessed with.

Robin medicine is hope, clarity, happiness, renewal, simplicity, satisfaction, new beginnings, a bright future, rejuvenation and celebration.

Seagull

One of my personal animal spirit guides, seagull always appears when I need to deal with my emotions or an emotional situation. The name seagull is a bit misleading (although it is a collective name for a huge family of gulls) as the seagull actually lives on land. Although you do find them at the seaside they are also just as happy in fresh water areas too. They are scavengers so they bring resourcefulness, adaptation and opportunity with them. Push yourself outside of your comfort zone to grab hold of opportunities that come your way. His scavenger ways remind us to value and make the most of what we have. His squawk is incredibly loud as he likes to be heard reminding us to shout if we need to have our voice heard and don't be afraid to speak your mind.

Seagull medicine is emotions, adapting, opportunity, communication, resourcefulness and freedom.

Spider

Don't be freaked out by this little guy, he is just doing his part in the grand scale of things. He is an ancient symbol of mystery as he weaves his web of life...with you at the centre. He is here to show us that we are all at the centre of our own webs and have the power to weave them in any way that we choose to. He brings us choices. Spiders also have eight legs and eight is the number for infinity; it symbolises the cycles of life and the passing of time.

Spider medicine is fate, death, feminine energy, cunning, cycles, rebirth, creation, protection, progression and resourcefulness.

Snail

Perhaps not the obvious choice when you think of seeking an animal guide, but seriously hear me out...probably the first thing you associate with snail is slime. But the slime has a purpose because it helps the snail to move forward and overcome obstacles. They also produce slime for protection, which also has healing properties too. Being both male and female, the snail also brings balance and perhaps the best of both worlds. The shell it carries on its back is home and it reminds us that home is wherever we make it.

Snail medicine is fertility, healing, protection, moving forward, changes, patience, cycles of life, self-reliance and self-assurance.

Snake

The snake is a very ancient symbol of the primordial life force, bringing the search for balance with him. Snake has both feminine energy on the creation and moon side, but also masculine energy on the power and healing side. It is the symbol of the never-ending cycle of life and one of healing powers. Snake also brings knowledge and cunning. As he sheds his skin he also symbolises transformation and leaving behind the old to look forward to the new.

Snake medicine is life cycles, patience, rebirth, fertility, balance, cunning, intuition, awareness, intellect, healing, protection, rejuvenation, transformation, hidden knowledge and duality.

Sparrow

We are probably all used to seeing sparrows and we perhaps often dismiss them as they are quite a common bird, but they pack a powerful punch of magic. Don't underestimate them. Sparrows are often seen in groups, which not only gives them protection, but also creates a community. She is always on the lookout for food and, in the breeding season, material for her nest, so brings productivity and hard work with her. Her life is simple and unburdened, but very rewarding. We could learn a lesson or two from her.

Sparrow medicine is creativity, protection, community, happiness, simplicity, productivity and friendship.

Squirrel

These happy little creatures like to have fun and it is a reminder to us to be less serious and get out and jump about, maybe not literally, but let your hair down occasionally. On the flip side he is also a very sensible chap and hides away food for the winter, so he also reminds us to be practical and put aside money for a rainy day and not to waste time, effort or food. Although apparently the squirrel often forgets where he has buried his stash of goodies, so make sure you are properly prepared and organised.

Squirrel medicine is energy, play, prudence, provision, forward planning, fun, balance, social, preparation and resourceful.

Worm

Aww even the poor ol' wriggly worm has animal medicine to share with us. He is a hardworking earth keeper who brings nourishment to the soil. He also brings respect for nature and the elements of the earth. He gives us warnings about looking after our environment.

Worm medicine is hard work, nourishment, nature, respect, the environment, transformation, productivity, fertility and emotions.

Wren

My little 'edge of the city' back garden gets regular bird visitors, but mostly of the larger variety – blackbirds, pigeons, magpies and the occasional seagull. Very rarely do we get any small birds, not even sparrows. So when I get a wren visitation I get silly excited (yes, I do need to get a life).

Wren represents a new phase of energy, increased activity and brings in more clarity to your mental and emotional vibes. There will also be an increase in your creative abilities and confidence to adapt to new situations.

Wren provides support and focus so that you can take a really good and honest look at what it is that you want and need. He will help you sift through the flotsam and jetsam and see what is what. He can also help bring clarity and insight to dreams and meditations. Wren also brings a new lease of life to relationships, whether they are work, home, family or friends.

Wren medicine is energy, activity, clarity, creativity, confidence, dreams, relationships, happiness, determination, strength, balance, resourcefulness, intuition and multitasking.

Journal Prompt
Jot down any animal sightings making a note of the date, time and place. Use your intuition and make a few notes detailing what meanings you think they have for you. Check back at a later date to see whether you were correct or not.

Chapter 22

Natural Rituals and Nature Deities

Sometimes I work with a ritual structure, especially if I am leading a group ritual. Something along the lines of casting the circle, calling the quarters, inviting deity then working magic and raising energy, then closing it all down in reverse. This format can work very well for wild witchcraft if you want it to. The elements are after all the basics of nature itself so inviting them in makes sense. Inviting deity to join you could be in the form of a specific goddesses and/or god that fits with your intent or perhaps a nature deity (see the list below). You may even choose to just invite Mother Earth and Father Sky to join you. And casting the circle can be done with natural items such as autumn leaves or flower petals. It really is all about working with your intuition and going with what feels right for you.

The alternative is to not plan any kind of structure, but just go with the flow. Stand in the middle of the forest, field or your garden and just see what happens...

If you are going to be raising energy or calling upon spirits it is often wise to cast a circle first, but you have to be guided by your intuition and your level of experience. Casting a circle only takes a moment and all you need is your visualisation skill to do it. If you are out in a natural setting it will be easy to make a physical circle with sticks, pebbles and leaves, but if you are in your living room at home then visualising is easier and less messy. If you are using just your imagination you can go wild with it; visualise a ring of leaves, a wall of sticks or even a moat, the options are endless. Casting a circle brings protection for you from without, but also to contain the energy that you raise within.

The act of casting a circle also helps to create your own

personal sacred space, but it is up to you to decide whether you need or want to do that. If you are in a sheltered glade in a forest or standing in a lonely spot on the moors you may already feel you are in a sacred space. Equally if you regularly work rituals and magic in your living room you may also feel that it is already your sacred space without need for anything further.

Representations of the elements in circle can be natural items such as a pebble for earth, a feather for air, a flame for fire (a candle in a lantern is probably the safest option) and a shell for water, but you don't need any physical items at all. Try calling in the elements and just visualising their properties and seeing if you can feel the energy and their presence; the wind on your face when calling east/air and the soil beneath your feet when calling north/earth, the moisture in the air or raindrops on your face for west/water and the sun on your skin when calling in south/fire.

You don't need any magical tools, you don't need any quarter representations, you don't need a wand or an athame. In fact, you don't need any tools or items at all. Just you, your intent and your imagination and you have yourself the most basic or elaborate ritual that you can conjure up in your mind's eye. The power is within *you* not any items or tools.

Journal Prompt

You can keep a record of any rituals that you perform, where and when and how you felt during and afterwards. But also, if any ideas pop into your mind just jot them down for use at a later date.

Nature Deities

I should probably mention that every witch will work with deity in a slightly different way and some won't work with deity at all, it is a very personal choice. The divine might be seen as Mother Earth and Father Sky or just the spirit in all things, or a person might work with individual deities. It is your journey so only you will know what works for you. However, I am going to look at some nature deities here because I personally work with individual gods and goddesses, although I do see them as parts of the whole. To me the goddess is like a big diamond and each different deity is a facet of that one diamond. They each have their own personality and character, but ultimately they are all a part of the one goddess.

This list is by no means comprehensive. but it is a start...

Flora and Fauna Deities

The Green Man/Jack-in-the-Green

Although the title 'Green Man' seems to be a fairly modern one, with a face created from foliage he appears as the all-encompassing male figure head of nature. He is also linked to the May Day celebrations and the pagan festival of Beltane. He guards the woodlands and the forests and all the animal and plant life therein.

He brings growth, new beginnings, fertility, truth, abundance and the cycle of death and rebirth.

Mother Nature

The life-giving, nurturing and creative force of nature. She is all.

She brings almost any magical intent that you can think of because she is the creator, caretaker and destroyer of all things.

Gaia

Gaia is the Greek goddess of the earth and one of the primordial elemental goddesses who was said to have been born at the dawn of creation. She is essentially the Greek version of Mother Nature as she is considered the mother of all creation. All heavenly deities were descended from her through various unions she had, with Uranus the sky, Pontos the sea and Gigantes the giants. Humans were conceived after an encounter with Tartarus the pit.

The Horned God

Perhaps a more modern definition of the male counterpart to the goddess, he may be a combination of several ancient gods such as Pan and Cernunnos. He is a strong and very masculine god with horns growing from his head. He embodies the woods, the forests and is guardian to the creatures. He is full of wisdom, strength, love, passion, sexuality, fertility and the energy of life...can I get a manly 'grrrrr'?

Pan

Greek god of the hunt and the wilds, he is said to be half human, but with the legs and horns of a goat. He can be found in nature settings, often near caves or mountains, and he is said to spend a lot of his time chasing nymphs in order to seduce them. By all accounts his chasing bears little or no results. He is also well known for playing music with his set of pipes. To me, Pan is a bit of a naughty old goat and although he is associated with nature and the good things that brings, he is also a bit of a handful and has a tendency to bring a heap load of chaos with him.

Cernunnos

The Celtic horned god, Cernunnos is associated with animals, particularly the stag, the hunt, the forests, fertility and plant life. He is considered to be Lord of the Forest and Master of the Hunt. In his guise as Master of the Hunt he pursues the souls of wrongdoers, guiding them to the Otherworld. He brings all aspects of nature, fertility, strength, protection, shape-shifting and the cycles of life.

Herne the Hunter

Herne is a keeper of the forest, but is usually associated with a specific area, that of the Forest of Windsor in Berkshire, England.

Many stories told of Herne involve him as a huntsman employed by King Richard II. One version of the story being that others in the court became jealous of Herne and his status and accused him of poaching. Falsely accused Herne became an outcast and in despair hung himself from an oak tree. Other tales tell that Herne saved King Richard from a charging stag and was himself injured in the process, but was miraculously cured by a passing stranger. That same stranger then demanded payment in the form of taking all of Herne's hunting skills. Herne was so bereft that he hung himself from the oak tree. Whatever version of the story, the tale says that his spirit still rides through the forests on a spectral hunt.

Aja

A Yoruban Orisha who carries the title 'Lady of Forest Herbs' and is said to teach the use of medicinal herbs to her followers. She also guards the forests and all the animals within. Also carrying the title of 'wild wind', it is believed that if you are swept away by her and then returned you will be a very powerful leader.

Artio

Artio is a Celtic bear goddess seeming to hail from the Helvetii, a tribe that migrated from Bavaria to Switzerland, which eventually became part of the Roman Empire. She appears throughout Gaul and Britain. She was worshipped as the 'she-bear' and looks after the harvest, fertility, abundance, wild animals, fruits and grains and journeying into the darkness.

Druantia

Druantia is a Celtic goddess and protector of trees and brings with her creativity, knowledge, passion, sexuality and the fertility of plants and animals. She is often referred to as 'Queen of the Druids'. Druantia guides the seekers to find knowledge and their true pathway and teaches the sacred ways of the forest.

Artemis

An Olympian goddess of the hunt, wild animals, the moon and the wilderness, she also covers the protection of children and childbirth. Often depicted carrying a bow and set of arrows, both the bear and deer are sacred to her. In fact, she owns a chariot that is drawn by two deer.

Cybele/Kybele

A goddess from Phrygian she was worshipped as the Mother of Gods and a primal nature goddess particularly associated with mountain regions. She is often connected with fertility and sexuality.

Demeter

An Olympian goddess of agriculture, grain and bread who keeps an eye on abundance from the earth. She is often depicted holding a sheaf of grain or a cornucopia and her sacred animals are the snake and the pig.

Aranyani

Aranyani is a Hindu goddess of the forests and guardian to all the animals that dwell within them. She is worshipped for fertility and the source of life.

Diana

A Roman goddess of wild animals and the hunt, but also a goddess of domestic animals and a fertility deity. Diana is also a moon goddess and one that protects women in childbirth. The oak is particularly sacred to her.

Faunus

As an ancient Italian deity, Faunus was a god of the countryside, the woodlands and forests and of abundance within the flocks and fields. Depicted as half man and half goat he is often equated with the Greek god Pan. The Roman celebration of Lupercalia involved honouring the god Faunus.

Gods of the Water

Tlaloc

Aztec god of thunder, rain and earthquakes. He could send rain or bring severe droughts and unleash lightning and hurricanes. Often depicted as a man wearing a net of clouds, a crown of heron feathers and foam sandals, he carries rattles that he uses to make thunder.

Chalchiuhtlicue

She is an Aztec goddess of all types of water, such as lakes, rivers, streams and storms. She brings fertility to crops and is often seen depicted in blues and greens with feathers in her hair.

Belisama

Ancient British goddess of lakes and rivers. She is also goddess of fire, crafts and light.

Manannan mac Lir

Irish god of the sea and ruler of the Otherworld and keeper of magic tools. He carries a magic spear and a crane bag, which is bottomless.

Mazu

Chinese goddess of water and protector of those travelling on the seas.

Anuket

Egyptian goddess of the Nile and provider of water for the fields, she was also seen as a goddess of the hunt and a protector of women during childbirth.

Tefnut

Egyptian goddess of water, dew, rain, mist, fertility and all things moist. She is associated with both the moon and the sun. She was known on the left representing the moon and moisture and on the right representing the sun and dryness. Her name means 'she of moisture'. Often depicted as a woman with a lion's head or as a lioness, she also occasionally took the form of a cobra.

Agwe

A sea loa; a water spirit who has a particular interest in seafarers. Ceremonies for Agwe are usually performed near the water and offerings floated on the water's surface. He is often depicted as a man dressed in naval uniform.

Vellamo

Finnish goddess of the sea, lakes and storms who is apparently quite moody.

Achelous

A Greek river god who was charged with caring for the largest river in Greece, the Eponymous, which made him the most important river god.

Amphitrite

Greek sea queen goddess and consort of Poseidon. She is the female personification of the sea and mother to all the fish and dolphins.

Poseidon

Greek Olympian god of the oceans and king of the sea gods, he also covers storms, floods, rivers, earthquakes and droughts.

Apah

Hindu goddesses of fresh water such as rivers and lakes. As

water goddesses, they cleanse and purify devotees. They bless them and grant immortality, energy and strength.

Sedna

Inuit goddess of the sea, she brings providence, nature, abundance and thankfulness. She is the mother of the sea and provides nourishment for the body and the soul. She is often depicted as having one eye that sees all things.

Suijin

Shinto god of water he guards fishermen, but also covers fertility, motherhood and childbirth in his remit.

Tangaroa

Maori god of the sea and one of the great gods, he is son of the sky and earth. He is the father of many sea creatures. Offerings are made to Tangaroa before any sea journey.

Nammu

Mesopotamian goddess of the primeval sea, she is the creatrix goddess and the source of water and fertility.

Njord

Norse god of the sea and one of the principal gods of the Vanir, he is also an honorary member of the Aesir gods. He is also associated with wealth and fertility as well as the sea and those who travel on it.

Aegir and Ran

Norse personification of the sea, they are husband and wife and live in a grand hall under the ocean. They are believed to control the power of the oceans, not only for good, but also the darker side of the ocean that causes shipwrecks and drowning.

Juturna

Turned into a water nymph by Jupiter, Juturna is a Roman goddess of wells, springs and fountains.

Neptune

Roman god of the sea, he is also associated with fresh water as well. Apparently very good looking with bright blue eyes and boundless energy, he also has a bad temper.

Yemaya

Yoruban Orisha of the ocean, Yemaya is considered to be mother of all things. She is the source of all waters and in fact her name means 'mother whose children are fish'. She brings fertility, wealth and protection for children.

Oshun

Yoruban Orisha of the rivers and fresh water. She brings healing to the sick along with fertility and prosperity. She is also an Orisha of love. In some stories she is said to have a fish tail like a mermaid.

Journal Prompt

If you work with any deities keep a record of who, when and what happened, how they came to you, how you worked with them and any messages they gave to you.

Chapter 23

Elementals

The elementals are the energies of nature itself; they are the forces of the elements. They are true energy and have the characteristics of the element they belong to. They can take on any shape, size or form to deal with a particular task.

Elementals can charge us with energy; they can work with us on a physical, mental, emotional and spiritual level. Learning to work with them can tune us in to connect with the energy of nature around us.

The elementals interweave their energy patterns to create and keep all of nature, all of life on our planet.

Elementals have nothing to obstruct them, they can move through matter with ease, but they also need to connect with us to help with their own spiritual growth and evolution.

You can help to connect with elementals by creating a natural incense from flower blossoms, leaves and seeds to burn. Use herbals that match the element of the elemental you wish to attract.

Earth Elementals – Gnomes

The gnome is the archetypal spirit of earth. Try not to think of the gnome you know from fairy tale stories, the elemental gnomes are very earthy, but their forms and shape can vary immensely and they can change to suit their situation.

Earth elementals maintain our planet, the structure itself. They create the forests, the trees, the plants and the flowers. They design all the crystals and rocks; they are very skilled craftsmen. They work very closely with nature. They are the beings that put the energy into all the rocks, pebbles and crystals.

An earth elemental can help us to attune to nature; they can work with us to help maintain our own physical bodies. They can help us develop all of our senses, to look after ourselves, to feel grounded and connected. Working with them can give us determination, appreciation, openness and spontaneity.

Be careful though, too much work with just the earth elemental and you might find yourself feeling cynical, sceptical and overly cautious.

Meditation to Connect with a Gnome

Make yourself comfortable.

Relax and let the worries and stresses of the day flow away.

Close your eyes and focus on your breathing, take deep breaths in and slow breaths out.

The world around you dissipates and you find yourself in a dark forest. The ground underfoot is deep, dark earth covered in leaf mulch. The air smells earthy and rich. Above you is a dense canopy of leaves. You don't feel afraid, in fact you feel very comfortable.

As you look around you notice the entrance to a small cave so you make your way over to it and peer inside.

In the distance you can see a light and hear sounds of movement. You are intrigued so you step into the cave entrance and head down the tunnel towards the light.

The walls of the cave are cold, but dry and the soil underfoot is compacted and obviously well-travelled.

As you come closer to the light source you realise that the walls of the cave tunnel are sparkling slightly. You stretch out your hand to touch the wall and feel geometric shapes. You realise that in fact the whole cave wall is covered in shining crystals.

Suddenly, the tunnel ends and opens out into a large cave...and it is breath-taking...crystals of all shapes, sizes and colours cover the walls and the ceiling.

You are interrupted from your crystal gazing by movement caught in the corner of your eye...

Turning you see a small figure, dressed in brown and dark green clothes with a mop of white hair and a wizened face underneath.

The figure speaks to you, asking your name and what you are seeking...

You find yourself talking easily to him without holding back...

When your conversation is finished, the figure reaches out and puts something in the palm of your hand and then bids you farewell.

You take one last look at the crystal cave and turn back towards the tunnel, making your way carefully out until you reach the forest once again.

Once outside you open your hand and look to see what gift you were given...

When you are ready come back to this reality, slowly open your eyes, shake your hands and stamp your feet.

Journal Prompt

Work with the meditation and make a note of any thoughts, feelings or messages you were given.

Water Elementals – Undines

These elementals are the force of water. It can be springs, rivers, oceans, lakes, wherever there is a source of natural water. Water is life, we can't survive without it. The water elementals can help us find our inner source, they can help us to find and work with our empathy, healing and purification.

Undines are a water sprite of sorts, more primal than a mermaid (or merman), but more developed than a basic water sprite – somewhere in between.

Undines work to keep our astral bodies in shape, to help us feel the connection to nature. They help us open up to our psychic abilities, our emotions, creativity, intuition and our imagination. They help us live life to the full and experience all that is available to us.

If you dream of water, the sea or rivers, that could be the undines at work. Ask for their help in dream work, they can aid you in lucid dreaming and astral travel.

Not connecting with the undines regularly can cause us to become unbalanced and we could find our bodies clogging up with toxins.

But again, be careful, as too much work with the undines can cause us to become overly emotional. On a physical level it can also manifest as water retention. You may become self-absorbed and your imagination might run away with you, making you overly sensitive and fearful.

Meditation to Meet an Undine

Make yourself comfortable.

Relax and let the worries and stresses of the day flow away.

Close your eyes and focus on your breathing. Take deep breaths in and slow breaths out.

As your world around you dissipates you find yourself sitting beside a clear blue pool of water. The colour is an amazing azure blue that sparkles in the sunlight.

It is a beautiful balmy day and the sun is warm on your body. As you look around you find you are in a paradise setting with swaying palm trees and multi-coloured birds and butterflies flying between the trees. The air is heavily scented with sweet flowers.

As you sit quietly your eye is drawn to the top of the pool and you watch as the sun glints on the surface and you realise that swimming just below are the most amazing fish...but suddenly there is a ripple in the water and a splash...

Right in front of you a creature has emerged from the water and is now sitting beside the pool looking at you. You are not afraid. The being is stunning to look at and you feel perfectly comfortable and at ease.

The creature asks your name and enquires as to whether you have any questions...

You find yourself opening up and talking with ease...

Once you are finished, the creature reaches out and puts something in the palm of your hand and then within the blink of an eye, a splash and ripple on the water, it has gone back beneath the surface.

You sit for a moment soaking up the warm sun, taking in the sweet scent of the air and then you open your hand to look at your gift...

When you are ready slowly come back to this reality, open your eyes and wriggle your fingers and toes.

Journal Prompt

Work with the meditation and make a note of any thoughts, feelings or messages you were given.

Air Elementals – Sylphs

These beings are the embodiment of air.

They are creativity; they are the source of life energy, what we might call prana or chi. We cannot live without air.

Sylphs are very intelligent; they create the atmosphere itself.

Sylphs do a lot of healing work. They can help to alleviate pain and ease suffering, but they also work to prompt inspiration and creativity. They work to help us fulfil our mental capacity to the fullest; they help us become inspired and seek knowledge. They clear out negative thoughts and keep our spirits up. They work with our intuition and our common sense.

Air elementals also care for our physical bodies by helping us to breathe.

As with all the elementals, too much exposure to sylphs can cause problems. It can make our minds overly active, we may procrastinate too much, we might become highly strung and extremely nervous, never settling on one thing and always wanting to change.

Meditation to Connect with a Sylph

Make yourself comfortable.

Relax and let the worries and stresses of the day flow away.

Close your eyes and focus on your breathing, take deep breaths in and slow breaths out.

As the world around you dissipates you find yourself sitting comfortably on the top of a mountain. The air is fresh and beautifully clean, but not cold. The sun is shining and there are wispy clouds streaked across a bright blue sky.

You are sitting on lush green grass that is scattered with pretty wild flowers. As you sit and look around you a tiny rabbit hops up and starts to nibble on a tuft of greenery near your feet, you sit and watch.

Then you start to feel a gentle breeze on your face, just very slightly ruffling your hair. Then a slightly stronger gust of wind brushes past you.

Turning you see a faint glimmer in the air, a wispy shape almost cloud like begins to strengthen and become more than an outline until there is a wavery figure standing before you, smiling.

You are not afraid. In fact you feel very comfortable and glad to be in the company of such a being.

The being asks your name and enquires as to whether you have any questions…

You find yourself talking quite freely and at length…

When you are finished, the being reaches forward and puts something in the palm of your hand.

Then as quickly as it came the being dissipates into the air and you are on your own again.

Take a few moments to look at your surroundings and then open your hand to see what the gift is that you have been given.

When you are ready, slowly come back to this reality, open your eyes and wriggle your fingers and toes.

Journal Prompt
Work with the meditation and make a note of any thoughts, feelings or messages you were given.

Fire Elementals – Salamanders

Salamanders are the embodiment of fire. Any flame has the spirit of fire elemental within it. They control all fires, all flames, lightning, heat, volcanoes and any explosions. They are also often attracted by the scent of cigarette or cigar smoke and the smell of alcohol.

Don't visualise a lizard-type creature, but think of a flame as it twists and turns like a serpent.

Fire elementals create very powerful emotions within us. They put the spark of spiritual ideas into our heads and hearts, they are the power that burns old habits and ideals and recreates new ones. Fire destroys and makes way for the new.

Fire elementals work with us for healing; they can detox the body. But we must be careful as their energy is very strong and not easy to control (think about a fire getting out of hand and how difficult it is to keep a check on). They also use their energy to help our spiritual selves. They work with our spiritual energy, they also stimulate our faith and enthusiasm and they open us up to psychic insight and perception. Working with the salamander can help with vitality and loyalty, making you assertive, spiritual and full of aspiration.

Not being connected with your fire elemental can cause lack of self-control, restlessness and burn-out, you can have impatience, distrust and pessimism. On a physical level, salamanders aid our circulation and body temperature, assisting our metabolism.

Meditation to Connect with a Salamander

Make yourself comfortable.

Relax and let the worries and stresses of the day flow away.

Close your eyes and focus on your breathing, take deep breaths in and slow breaths out.

As your world around you dissipates you find yourself sitting on the sand. The sun is very hot and the air around you is dry, but you are not uncomfortable.

As you look at your surroundings you realise you are in a desert with sand and bleached yellow rocks all around you.

In the distance you can see a few scrawny plants trying to survive in the dry heat of the desert.

Turning around you see a large outcrop of rocks that appear to be providing some shade, so you make you way over.

You climb carefully under the ledge of the largest rock and sit down in the coolness of the shade.

As you sit and look out at the barren scenery you hear movement to the side of you. You turn to see a creature now basking in the sun on one of the flat rocks. As it soaks up the blazing heat it turns and looks at you.

The creature asks your name and whether you have any questions...

You find yourself talking to the creature as if it were your best friend...

When you are finished talking the creature puts something in the palm of your hand and bids you farewell. Then with a scuffle of movement it is gone.

You take a moment to think about your conversation and then open your hand to see what your gift was.

When you are ready come back to this reality, open your eyes and wriggle your fingers and toes.

Journal Prompt

Work with the meditation and make a note of any thoughts, feelings or messages you were given.

Chapter 24

Dragon Magic

Dragon magic is an ancient and fascinating subject and one that covers so much that I couldn't possibly fit it all in just this section, but hopefully what I have tried to do here is cover the basics and maybe whet your appetite just a little. Being out in the wilds, whether it is in a forest or a city, you may well stumble on some dragon magic.

There are different views of what dragons are and represent. They are sometimes viewed as mythological entities that represent a set of principles.

A dragon viewed as a winged serpent could be a symbol of the earth and the Underworld. The wings can be seen as a symbol of the heavens. The winged serpent brings together these two principles – as above, so below.

The Chinese dragon is a symbol of Tao, that which is beyond all terms and all polarities, but also the force behind all (Yin and Yang).

The dragon represents the unknown, the hidden energy in humans and in nature.

The word dragon comes from the Greek verb 'derkein', which means 'to see'. The dragon is the principle of clear seeing: the ability to see things in a new light as they really are, beyond all illusions.

You might be familiar with the idea of a dragon hording his treasure (think of Smaug in his cave in *The Hobbit*). It is that treasure that symbolises the wisdom it keeps. To enable us to find the knowledge that a dragon guards we have to look within and maybe even tread into some uncomfortable corners of our inner self to find the answers. Hey, I never said that working with dragons was easy...

If you have ever practised yoga you will know the dragon as the Kundalini, the force that is hidden inside us. We all have it within us to awaken the forces of the dragon.

The world of dragons has so many different breeds, types, colours, sizes and shapes. Some you may be more familiar with than others – the Chinese or the Welsh dragon for instance, others such as wyrm may be new to you. But, no matter what they look like, they all hold incredible power.

A dragon can be a strong, useful and wise totem or guardian and we can also tap into dragon energy to use within our rituals and our magic.

Dragons are a primeval force, they are physical and spiritual, they bring with them the full force and power of the elements. They are also very wise and intelligent.

If you are an experienced witch or light worker you should be very used to using energy and maybe even sensing energy fields. If you pick up the feeling of a large energy field around you then it might be a dragon.

Whether dragons did roam the earth at one time, I don't know; I like to think so. But now they exist in the astral and spiritual plane.

Dragon energy is one of the most powerful energies I know of and when blended together via the four main elements, creates the etheric dragon...a super power, just without the cape.

Dragon energy is linear, so be careful what you ask for. You will receive it in the most direct way possible. Be very specific about your intentions, integrity and intelligence. Dragons do not necessarily use human logic. If you offer them a problem they will find a solution, but it will be a straightforward one, removing anything in its path to solve it...

Dragon energy is very good at removing dark energy, it is good for clearing negative energy, but make sure you also ask for positive vibes to be left in its place. And I have found it is always best to end your request with 'and do no harm'. Dragon magic works quickly and can sometimes have unexpected results.

As witches usually have an element we favour to work with, I have found that dragons do too. Not everyone believes that we have 'elemental dragons' as such, they aren't necessarily made up from one particular element, it is just that they work best with one element, although you will also find a few that work well with all the elements. These are particularly powerful.

While I don't want to put you off working with dragons, I would ask you to remember that these are very old and very wise creatures. They also have a tendency to get bored easily and are impatient. (Sounds just like me…) So always treat them with the respect that you would a wise elder.

What I can tell you is that working with dragon energy can be very beneficial and a wonderful experience. Dragons also have so much to teach us; all that ancient wisdom waiting to be shared, not to mention all the powerful energy and support that they can provide us with.

And a word about the chaos dragon, which is usually dark purple in colour and really a bit of a mischief maker. Just keep an eye on him and you will be fine. He is, however, extremely useful to call upon when you need to undo a spell.

Dragon Lines

I talked about ley lines earlier in this book – the magnetic fields of energy that form lines crossing and intersecting over the earth. Centuries ago the Chinese called ley lines 'dragon lines'. When the dragon lines cross each other their energy spirals and becomes a vortex. If several lines cross at a certain point (a node) it can produce a huge vortex of energy.

Dragon Healing

Dragon energy is very useful for healing; you can channel it when using crystal healing or in hands-on healing, but there is also a form of Reiki that combines dragon energy too, for the purpose of healing.

Dragons in Ritual

You can call upon dragons in your quarter calls, as you would call in the elements.

Dragon Sprit Guide/Guardian

Having a dragon spirit guide is very special; they are incredibly powerful and wise.

If dragon appears as your guide it usually means you need one or some of their qualities, such as strength or courage. They also bring the message of balance and ask us to use our psychic abilities to see the world as magical.

Once dragon has come to you, I do encourage you to connect with it on a regular basis. Make a connection and keep it. A dragon spirit is very useful, not only as a powerful guardian, but also as a guide – keep it happy.

There are many ways to strengthen your bond with your dragon guide. Here are a few suggestions:

- Meditate upon your dragon spirit.
- Collect dragon images – statues, pendants or pictures.
- Read everything you can on dragons, including all the fairy tales, myths and legends. This will not only strengthen your connection, but also expand your knowledge.

The dragon spirit guide possesses the following energies: leadership, magical prowess, vitality, mastery, insight, divine illumination, protection from outside evil forces from all directions, grounded energy, fulfilment of potential, inspiration, longevity, personal happiness, greatly increased riches, infinite wisdom, luminous beauty, majesty, indomitable spirit and strength, invisibility, power of transformation and metaphysical knowledge.

In Celtic Tradition

The fire dragon is a symbol of transmutation, energy and mastery. If this is your spirit guide you will be given enthusiasm, courage and vitality. Your inner fire will be fuelled. You will be helped to overcome obstacles. You will be given the qualities of leadership and mastery. The fire dragon can also be a strong protector.

The air dragon brings insight, inspiration and vitality. This spirit guide must be handled with the greatest of respect. Insight, wisdom and clarity will be given for all problems. As always – trust your inner voice.

The earth dragon brings potential, power and riches. You will be shown your potential and exactly what you are capable of. With the earth dragon's assistance, you may discover the beauty and power that lies within you and within us all. The earth dragon resides deep within the Earth and can aid you in grounding. He will nurture you like Mother Earth does.

The water dragon brings connection, depth and passion. The water dragon as a spirit guide brings memories and wishes, perhaps long forgotten yet hidden, to the fore. By facing up to painful past experiences, a sense of peace and balance can be achieved. The water dragon will give you the courage and compassion.

Dragon Types

Below are just a few descriptions of some of the many dragon types.

Chinese dragons (Chinese: lóng or 'lung') are typically portrayed as long, scaled, serpentine creatures with four legs. Chinese dragons traditionally symbolize potent and auspicious powers, particularly control over water, rainfall, and floods. In yin and yang terminology, a dragon is yang (male) and complements a yin (female) fenghuang 'Chinese phoenix'.

Japanese dragon myths amalgamate native legends with imported stories about dragons from China, Korea and India.

Like these other Asian dragons, most Japanese ones are water deities associated with rainfall and bodies of water, and are typically depicted as large, wingless, serpentine creatures with clawed feet.

European dragons are often referred to as a wyrm or wurm. This terminology can be confusing as wyrms are also described as a type of dragon with a long slender body, often able to breathe fire, with either none or four limbs, but usually without wings. The word derives from the Old Germanic 'Gewurm'.

In European folklore, a dragon is a serpentine legendary creature. The Latin word draco, as in constellation Draco, comes directly from Greek δράκων, (drákōn, gazer). The word for dragon in Germanic mythology and its descendants is worm (Old English: wyrm, Old High German: wurm, Old Norse: ormr), meaning snake or serpent. In Old English wyrm means 'serpent', draca means 'dragon'.

Finnish lohikäärme means directly 'salmon-snake', but the word lohi- was originally louhi- meaning crags or rocks, a 'mountain snake'. Though a winged creature, the dragon is generally to be found in its underground lair, a cave that identifies it as an ancient creature of earth.

In western folklore, dragons are often portrayed as evil. In modern times the dragon is typically depicted as a huge fire-breathing, scaly and horned dinosaur-like creature, with leathery wings, four legs and a long muscular tail. It is sometimes shown with feathered wings, crests, fiery manes, spikes running down its spine and in various exotic colours.

In Celtic mythology, the dragon was considered a benevolent dweller of caves, lakes and the inner earth. In ancient times, it was a symbol of wealth and associated with the power of the elements (particularly that of the earth), but also of the subconscious mind. Dragons often appeared in many varieties: as water serpents or worm-shaped beasts as well as the more well-known winged depiction. The dragon represented the supernatural forces that guarded the great secrets and treasures of the universe.

Dragon Meditation

Make yourself comfortable in a place where you won't be disturbed.

Close your eyes and focus on your breathing.

Your world around you dissipates and you find yourself in a clearing. In the distance you can see mountains and what looks like a volcano top with smoke creeping out of its crater. Behind you is a large dense forest and to one side you turn to see a large lake.

Look up towards the sky and see the storm clouds rolling in from over the mountain tops, although the sun is still trying to break through and long shafts of light beam down on the surface of the lake making it glint and sparkle.

You realise you are not alone. Flying high above you are shapes that appear as large birds, but on a second look you realise they are dragons, dark shapes weaving in and out of the clouds. Then you hear crashing sounds coming from the forest and realise that behind the trees large dragons are moving around. But you don't feel afraid.

Splashing from the lake draws your attention and you notice that some of the glints in the water are actually dragons swimming, ripples breaking the surface of the water.

A loud roaring sound draws your attention to the mountain tops and you see that diving in and out of the volcano crater are dragons, breathing long streams of flame as they dive.

Then on the shoreline of the lake you realise what you thought were sandy rocks are in reality, huge desert dragons sunning themselves.

Stand for a moment and draw on the powers of all these different dragons. Reach out with your mind and see if one of them makes a connection with you.

If one does, ask it to join you where you are standing. Wait until it stands beside you then ask for permission to ask it some questions. If it agrees, then ask what you want to know.

Once you are finished, thank the dragon for its presence, guidance and wisdom and bid it farewell. It may tell you that it is your dragon guardian now and you can call upon it any time, but it may not.

Know that you can always come back to the land of dragons for guidance.

Slowly bring your focus back to the present, shake your arms and legs and open your eyes.

Journal Prompt

Work with the meditation and make a note of any thoughts, feelings or messages you were given.

Chapter 25

Natural Crafts

Mother Nature provides us with all sorts of items that can be used in magical workings, but also those that can be turned, with just a little bit of effort, into beautiful and/or useful crafts. Here are some ideas to get you started:

Journey Stick

A journey stick is a tool that you create yourself from a small branch or large stick. It can be any size to suit you, from small wand to large staff. Your stick is decorated with items that are symbolic to you and your pathway and can have representations of the elements, deities you work with or just gifts from nature such as feathers, stones or shells. Tie each item to the stick with leather thong, twine or ribbon. You can also carve symbols or sigils into the wood itself. The journey stick can then be held to help you as you meditate, hedge ride or journey and can be used to channel energy for spell work. Be creative.

Forest Twig Candle Holders

Get the feel of the forest by creating woodland candleholders.

You will need
A glass or clean jam jar
Twigs
Glue – a strong craft adhesive or a hot glue gun

The instructions are simple...glue the twigs around the glass; you could finish off by tying a ribbon or piece of rustic twine around.

Twig Photo/Picture Frame

A variation on the above; stick twigs around a plain photo frame – you can purchase photo frames cheaply in thrift/charity stores or discount stores.

Glue the twigs using craft adhesive or a hot glue gun. Pop a photo in the frame.

Element Pebbles

Paint pebbles or shells with images of the four elements. Use your own designs or go with more traditional ones.

Faerie Bells

These are so easy to make and sound lovely hanging in the garden.

You will need
Sticks
Wool, cord or thread
Bells
Beads
Ribbons

Wrap coloured thread or wool around a stick, tie on bells and beads and bits of ribbon then hang them in the garden...simples.

Sea Shell Mosaic Pictures

You can create all sorts of images with sea shells.

You will need
Sea shells (obviously...)
Craft glue
Stiff card or a piece of wood to stick them to.

Lay out the design first then glue each shell in place.

Beach in a Jar

These are really fun to create and make a connection to the ocean in your home.

You will need
A mason jar or large jam jar
Sand
Shells
Sea glass
Driftwood
Any natural items you find on the beach that are small enough to pop into the jar.

Fill the jar a quarter to half full with sand then add in your shells and other items.

Witches' Ladder

Cut nine pieces of natural twine or ribbon (or a mixture of both), about 1 metre in length.

If you are going to use ribbon, then think about colour too. Pick the colour to match the intent of your witches' ladder.

Gather together three strands and tie a knot in one end, then begin to plait them together, tying a knot at the other end when you have finished.

Repeat with the other strands until you have three sets of three plaited lengths. Then you are going to plait these together.

While you are working focus on your intent, maybe even chant as you go.

If you are really crafty you can add in beads, charms or other embellishments as you plait. Or, if you are like me, sew them on afterwards.

Once you have completed the plait, make sure it is secure at both ends. Then at regular intervals poke in a feather or piece of herb between the braiding. As you do this, focus on the intent.

Place your finished witches' ladder on your altar or put it where you will see it every day until your purpose has come to fruition.

Candles

You can decorate candles with all sorts of things:

- Dress them in oil and roll them in crushed herbs.
- Tie them with ribbon.
- Use dress-making pins pushed into the candle.
- Stick pressed flowers or dried leaves onto the outside with a dab of melted wax.
- Pop a candle into a jar filled with lavender, lentils, rice or coffee beans.
- Fill a bowl with water, shells and pebbles and float candles on the top.

Apple Candle Holders

What you need
Firm apples or even small squashes
Lemon juice
Herbs of your choice
Taper candles

Rinse the fruit or vegetable and dry them. Give the outside a bit of a polish to make it clean and shiny. Using a knife or a corer, make a hole in the top where the stem is. Work down about halfway into the fruit so that the candle will have a firm base. Make the hole the same diameter as your candle. Pour some lemon juice into the hole and let it sit for a few minutes, this helps stop the fruit from going brown and squishy too quickly. Pour out the lemon juice and then dry the inside. Insert a sprig of fresh herbs into the hole; rosemary or thyme works well. Then take your taper candle and drip a small amount of wax into the hole to secure the candle and quickly set the candle in it.

Chimes

You will need
Chime objects such as bottle tops, little bells, shells, glass, beads, wooden shapes etc.
Chime lid – Something to hang the chimes from
String
A drill (optional) and safety goggles may be needed

Make holes in your chime objects and the lid. Please be really careful if you are using a drill.

Tie string through your chime objects.

Attach the objects to your lid.

Hang where it will catch a nice breeze.

Sit, relax and listen to the calming sounds made by your new wind chime. Perhaps even have a cup of tea and a slice of cake.

Loose Incense

I am sure most of us use incense in one form or another and it is really easy to make, especially the loose incense that you burn on a charcoal disc. Or, if you don't want to burn it, you can also use loose incense as pot pourri.

Start with a base. A resin is good such as frankincense or copal. Adding a wood of some sort helps your incense to burn longer too, something like sandalwood, or if you are using home-grown dried herbs the woody stems of herbs can be added too. Then the choice is up to you, whether you go for the scent you like or for the intent. Incense can be made for prosperity, love, success and so on, but you can also make incense to correspond with the moon phase, a sabbat, a particular ritual or to honour a specific deity.

I also like to add a few drops of essential oil to my incense mix once I have finished it as well, just to give it an extra boost of scent and power.

Remember that incense put together for magical purpose may not always smell particularly pleasant; it is the energies of the herbs that are important.

I would also suggest keeping it simple. Add too many ingredients and it gets complicated. Less is more as they say.

Pick your base resin and/or wood, tying them into your intent, then add herbs, spices and flowers – keep them corresponding to your intent. If you are making an incense to represent the element of air you would choose herbs that relate to that element, such as anise, lavender and mint perhaps. If you were making incense to honour the Goddess you might use lemon balm, geranium and thyme as these are all feminine herbs.

Don't forget that loose incense burnt on charcoal makes quite a bit of smoke, especially if you have included a resin.

Medicine Bags

Medicine bags, gris gris or mojo bags are fabulous to work with. (All are different names for pretty much the same thing.)

A medicine bag contains items that are charged with your intent and each item is a guide for the spirits to help them understand what outcome you desire. Your medicine bag, once it is put together, is essentially 'alive' with energy and it will need to be looked after and can be 'fed' with magic powder. You will need to feed or charge it periodically to maintain its energy force.

The African's call the power of nature 'ashe' and this is what is present in all herbs, plants, stones – in fact anything from nature. It is this power that we are using within the medicine bags.

A medicine bag can contain all sorts of items: herbs, roots, spices, crystals, feathers, bones, shells, dirt, pebbles and coins –

what you put in your medicine bag is up to you.

Traditional gris gris bags use red flannel for the bag itself, but I like to add colour magic to my medicine bags. I use orange material a lot as this is the colour for success, but also green for prosperity and blue for healing works really well. You don't even have to be good at sewing, use a handkerchief (do people still use these?), or felt is good as that doesn't need hemming, or just use a scrap of material. They can be tied with string or ribbon. You can also use the chiffon bags that craft shops sell for wedding favours.

Magic Powder

And now onto the magic powder to feed your medicine bag – although magic powders also have lots of other uses. They can be used to roll candles in for spell work, to sprinkle around your house for protection, to add oomph to rituals and any spells, to add to poppets and witch bottles or to wear in a small bottle as a charm.

To make a magic powder the ingredients you use must be ground, so you will need either a pestle and mortar or the end of a rolling pin and a solid bowl.

As you add each ingredient to the bowl, charge it first with your intent. I also like to charge the powder as a whole once it is complete too.

This can then be fed to your medicine bag each week, just a sprinkle. You can even boost the power by feeding it on the corresponding day of the week to your intent. Or keep it in an airtight bottle or jar and use it for all sorts of other spell work.

I like to use a base for my magic powders. I usually work with either salt or sugar, as it grinds well and adds its own qualities to the mix. If I am making faerie wishes powder I also like to add in a little bit of glitter obviously (if you are using the magic powder outside, please use edible glitter).

Use a suitable chant as you grind the powder together with

your intent.

Witches' Bottles

I love using witch bottles. I always have at least two on the go in my house for protection, clearing out negative energies and bringing happiness to the home.

These are so easy to make. You don't need special pretty bottles, you can just use old clean jam jars.

Generally speaking, modern day witch bottles are very similar to historical witch bottles in their basic structure, even though their intended purpose has changed. The most common purpose for constructing a witch bottle today is to capture negative energy and send it back out as positive energy.

The basic structure of witch bottles can be used for purposes other than protection, such as prosperity, healing and love.

Basically, a witch bottle is a container of some sort, usually a jar or a bottle, which is filled with objects that correspond to a given intent. The items are magically charged as they are added and can also be recharged with energy for as long as is needed, provided the bottle does not get broken.

Traditionally a witch bottle would have contained nails, earth, stones, knotted threads, herbs, spices, resin, flowers, candle wax, salt, vinegar, oil, coins, ashes and quite often urine.

Originally witch bottles were used to keep witches away. They also used to contain all sorts of bodily fluids, hair and finger nail clippings – you can add these if you want to.

Start with your jar or bottle, then charge each item before you add it, layering up the 'ingredients' as you go.

It really is up to you what you put in. I like to put in three nails to attract negativity and for protection, I also put in a piece of string with three knots, knotting in my intent with each tie. If it is for prosperity I often drop in a silver coin. I usually put salt in for protection, cleansing and purification. I also like to add some kind of dried pulse – lentils or beans to 'soak' up any negative energy. Garlic is good for protection too. Then add any herbs, spices and flowers that correspond with your intent – rose petals for love, cinnamon for success, mint and basil for prosperity etc. Keep filling the jar or bottle up until you reach the top, then put the lid on. If I am using a jam jar I like to draw a pentacle on the lid. If I am using a bottle with a cork I like to seal the cork lid with dripped wax.

If I am making the witch bottle for protection for my own home I like to put in a pebble from the garden, a couple of fallen leaves from the tree in my yard and a bit of cobweb from inside the house. It makes it all more personal and ties the bottle to the energies of the home.

Poppets

I love these little guys (or gals). It is a shame they have had so much bad press.

When most people think of a poppet, they automatically think of the Voodoo doll, thanks to this item's negative portrayal in movies and on television. However, the use of dolls in sympathetic magic goes back several millennia. Back in the days of ancient Egypt, the enemies of Ramses III (he had a lot) used wax images of the Pharaoh, to bring about his death.

It wasn't uncommon for the Greeks to use sympathetic magic in workings related to love or war. Greek poppets called Kolossoi were sometimes used to restrain a ghost or even a dangerous deity, or to bind two lovers together.

I like to think of a poppet as a person-shaped spell holder and I use them for love, luck, protection, prosperity and healing or just about any intent that is needed.

Remember that poppets have a long tradition behind them, and that tradition is influenced by the magical practices of a wide range of cultures. Treat your poppets well, and they will do the same for you.

As for design, well it's really up to you. You can make a

simple poppet from twine, grasses or ivy tied together right up to detailed material poppets with hair and glass eyes and, of course, anything in between. You can even use dollies or Barbie dolls.

I like to use felt when making poppets, basically because I am a lazy sewer. With felt you don't have to hem. And, of course, felt comes in all sorts of colours so you can correspond the colour of felt used to the intent.

I cut out two felt shapes, a bit like a gingerbread man or a 'T' shape.

Then I sew a button on for one eye and a cross for the other eye, followed by a mouth. Then I sew on a little red felt heart.

Next I sew with neat, but not fancy, stitches around the edges of the figure. Again you can use coloured thread to correspond with your intent.

I leave a gap and then stuff the poppet with some off-cuts of felt, but also herbs and spices; occasionally I will add a crystal too. You can use all sorts of herbs, woods, plants, roots and spices even salt and rice – go with what suits your intent or what feels right for you. Salt, rice and dried pulses are good if your poppet is larger as they fill up the space nicely and also work for purification, protection, negative energy and, in the case of rice, prosperity too. Charge each item as you add it. Then when your poppet is full sew it up. I like to charge mine with my intent again once they are whole.

I set my poppets on my altar and recharge them occasionally with my intent.

Some people choose to bury poppets once they are made, allowing the universe to work the magic but please make sure they are made from biodegradable fabric and fillings.

Journal Prompt

Keep a notebook just for the crafts that you make, detail anything that you create, why, when, what you put in it and how well it worked. Especially when making something like incense or magic powder it helps to see what ingredients worked well and what didn't so that you can improve on the recipe next time.

Chapter 26

Hedge Riding

I have written about hedge riding in one or two of my other books, but I think it is really important to include it here for the witch going into the wilds.

The hedge is the symbolic boundary between the worlds. Hedge riding is the journey your spirit takes into the Otherworld or Underworld realms, sometimes called the upper and lower realms. The middle realm being our everyday world that we live in.

Hedge riding can take our spirit travelling back into the past to connect with our ancestors and we can meet and talk with our past-life selves. The upper realm can provide us with connections to our spirit guides, teachers and the Divine. The lower realm takes us on a journey to find animal guides and to meet the souls of those who have passed over.

Hedge riding is not something to be taken lightly; it definitely isn't somewhere to just visit because you are bored. It is something to be taken very seriously and journeys should be focused with a particular question or mission in mind. It might be a journey undertaken for the purposes of healing, seeking an answer to a question, for spell work or to find spiritual enlightenment.

Personally, I would advise becoming experienced in pathworking, shape shifting and astral travel before attempting to hedge ride, not purely for safety, but also because it will help you with the journey. This is not something to be attempted by those just stepping onto the meditation ladder. Hedge riding should also be avoided if you are feeling unwell or if you have any kind of mental illness.

Hedge riding is very similar to shamanic journeys and also incorporates the art of Seidh or 'seer work' in that you will communicate with the spirits.

During a journey your spirit, your conscious, will travel to the Otherworld and while there you will need to take note of any symbols or signs that you see and any sounds you hear or scents you smell. They may all be important.

A witch will enter the Otherworld via a trance state, which is an altered state of consciousness when your mind and spirit work separately from your physical body. You are not fully conscious, but you are not unconscious. You are in that wonderful state in between, but you are always fully aware of what you are doing. You are lucid and in control, but don't fall asleep.

Altered states of consciousness can be induced via means of drugs, but I would wholeheartedly *not* advise this route. You will need to go past the state of meditation and on to pathworking to achieve hedge riding. I find drumming helps, but chanting can also be very useful. Shamanic music with drums and rattles is also good; any rhythmic beat will work well.

Keep a notebook with you when your hedge ride, then you can jot down anything that you saw or heard as soon as you come back to reality, because it has a habit of slipping away once you get up and move about. I recommend writing down absolutely everything, even the small details.

Hedge riding equipment – you don't *need* anything, just your mind, but you can use a few bits and bobs to help your journey along.

Rattles and drums can be used to get you into a trance state, as I have mentioned above, but they can also help to clear away any negative energy, call to the spirit guides and help bring in healing energies. I would also advise smudging your room before you begin any journey.

Many witches have a medicine bag that they use to keep magical items in to aid in journeying. Each bag will be personal and specific to the individual. It might contain beads, shells, feathers, pebbles, herbs and crystals – if you decide to make your own bag, be guided by your intuition and add whatever you feel is necessary to help you on your hedge riding.

Ointments – you have all probably read or heard about flying ointments. These did actually exist and were usually made from all sorts of nasty and quite often fatal ingredients, and personally I would avoid them. It is really not worth taking a chance. Instead of an ointment you can use incense blended with herbs and natural items that correspond to contacting the spirit world, Otherworld and to aid in psychic abilities.

An animal spirit guide is extremely useful to journey to the other side of the hedge with. In my experience you don't choose your animal guide, it chooses you. Don't be surprised if your hedge riding guide is a different one from your usual power animal and you may also find that your guide to the different worlds will be different in each one. They might even be different for each journey you take or you may have the same guide every time...be open to whatever you meet.

You might find that it takes a few hedge riding journeys before you meet any spirit guides and you may find different guides in each world. They may be there to guide you, they may be there to give you a message, but it won't always be via spoken word, look out for signs and symbols.

The Three Realms

Let's talk about the three realms that a witch can enter...and I am going to describe the general ideas, but...your experience may be different.

Generally (not always) a witch will access the worlds via a tree, often it is seen as the Tree of Life and it is a portal to the Otherworld. You might see an entrance between the roots that takes you to the Lower World, there might be an entrance halfway up the trunk to the Middle World and an entrance in the upper branches to the Upper World – what you see might be different. There is also another level accessed via the Lower

World, this takes you down another level to the Underworld. How you see it might be different to this description, you might access all worlds via the same tunnel that splits in different directions or you might access it through another portal other than a tree...

The Underworld/Hades/Tir na n-Og/Helheim

The Underworld or the Lower World as it is sometimes called is not a deep, dark fiery hell pit...really it isn't. It can, however, be seen as darker than the Middle World. It may often appear as a cave or a primordial jungle. You can find dangers in the Underworld, but you can also meet them in the Middle and Upper World too. The Underworld is earthy, stable and grounding; it is the base from which the world grows. The Underworld deals with emotions, our intuition and our very basic needs. You may meet ancestors there, animal guides, guardians, plant spirits and the Underworld kings and queens along with the Faerie realm are found here. If you are experienced in hedge riding, this is also the place to do soul retrieval.

The Middle World/Earth/Midgard/Bith

The Middle World is often used as a place for time travel (you are thinking Doctor Who now and his Tardis aren't you?). The Middle World is very much like our own and you can find yourself in any familiar type of structure, building or landscape. This world is as much full of bad spirits as it is good, so be wary. You will find earth and fertility deities here along with the elementals, land guardian spirits, messenger deities, nature spirits and the Wild Hunt.

The Upper World/Avalon/Asgard/Olympus

This world is beeeeautiful. Spirits live here and it shows. Think beautiful landscapes, dreamy clouds, sparkling streams and all that is amazing. This is the place to meet and greet spirit guides, angels, ascended masters, devas, deities and animal guides. It is the upper astral, the spiritual plane and a place of enlightenment. This world will show you knowledge, inspiration, ideas and wisdom (hopefully) and also provide healing. The Upper World can also help you remove yourself from your ego and see things as they really are.

For Your Ride

You may want to cast a circle before you journey. I don't, but it is your personal choice. You may prefer to just cast a personal shield of protective light around yourself before you start. Make sure you are comfortable, and remember that sitting still for any period of time lowers your body temperature, so you might want a shawl or a blanket to hand. I like to smudge the room first and light some incense. I also prefer the lighting low and some candlelight. You may want to sit and hold your medicine pouch if you have one or a crystal to help focus you. I also like to play a CD with shamanic drumming or singing bowls to help alter my conscious.

Don't forget it is very wise to ground and centre before *and* after any journeying.

Before you start your hedge ride make sure you have an idea of what your purpose and intent is, whether it is a question you need an answer to, advice on a situation or healing. Throughout your journey keep focused on your intent.

If you are looking for answers, take note of any symbols you see, objects you find, people or animals you meet. You may also come across pools of water that can be used for scrying.

Healing can be achieved by bathing in oceans, streams or pools or you can use the energy from your animal guides to help the healing process. Your guides can also help with protection requirements.

Your spirit guides in the Upper World can help you out if you are seeking knowledge.

Please remember to always be polite and courteous to any animal or being that you meet in any of the worlds – treat them with respect at all times.

If you should meet any spirit that you don't like, politely but firmly ask them to leave – you have the power to make it leave… you are in complete control.

Journal Prompt

I believe it is always advisable to make notes after any journey or meditation of any kind because it doesn't take long for my mind to forget what happened. Any small detail may be really important and it is useful to note it all down so that you have a reference to look back over afterwards.

Into the Wilds and Back Again

This is your journey and it will be a very personal one, your pathway may twist and turn and take diversions on the way, but ultimately it is yours to take. Trust your intuition and be guided by your inner voice…the journey has just begun.

MOON
BOOKS

Moon Books

PAGANISM & SHAMANISM

What is Paganism? A religion, a spirituality, an alternative belief system, nature worship? You can find support for all these definitions (and many more) in dictionaries, encyclopaedias, and text books of religion, but subscribe to any one and the truth will evade you. Above all Paganism is a creative pursuit, an encounter with reality, an exploration of meaning and an expression of the soul. Druids, Heathens, Wiccans and others, all contribute their insights and literary riches to the Pagan tradition. Moon Books invites you to begin or to deepen your own encounter, right here, right now. If you have enjoyed this book, why not tell other readers by posting a review on your preferred book site. Recent bestsellers from Moon Books are:

Journey to the Dark Goddess
How to Return to Your Soul
Jane Meredith
Discover the powerful secrets of the Dark Goddess and transform your depression, grief and pain into healing and integration.
Paperback: 978-1-84694-677-6 ebook: 978-1-78099-223-5

Shamanic Reiki
Expanded Ways of Working with Universal Life Force Energy
Llyn Roberts, Robert Levy
Shamanism and Reiki are each powerful ways of healing;
together, their power multiplies. Shamanic Reiki introduces
techniques to help healers and Reiki practitioners tap ancient
healing wisdom.
Paperback: 978-1-84694-037-8 ebook: 978-1-84694-650-9

Pagan Portals – The Awen Alone
Walking the Path of the Solitary Druid
Joanna van der Hoeven
An introductory guide for the solitary Druid, The Awen Alone
will accompany you as you explore, and seek out your own
place within the natural world.
Paperback: 978-1-78279-547-6 ebook: 978-1-78279-546-9

A Kitchen Witch's World of Magical Herbs & Plants
Rachel Patterson
A journey into the magical world of herbs and plants, filled
with magical uses, folklore, history and practical magic. By
popular writer, blogger and kitchen witch, Tansy Firedragon.
Paperback: 978-1-78279-621-3 ebook: 978-1-78279-620-6

Medicine for the Soul
The Complete Book of Shamanic Healing
Ross Heaven
All you will ever need to know about shamanic healing and
how to become your own shaman...
Paperback: 978-1-78099-419-2 ebook: 978-1-78099-420-8

Shaman Pathways – The Druid Shaman
Exploring the Celtic Otherworld
Danu Forest
A practical guide to Celtic shamanism with exercises and techniques as well as traditional lore for exploring the Celtic Otherworld.
Paperback: 978-1-78099-615-8 ebook: 978-1-78099-616-5

Traditional Witchcraft for the Woods and Forests
A Witch's Guide to the Woodland with Guided Meditations and Pathworking
Melusine Draco
A Witch's guide to walking alone in the woods, with guided meditations and pathworking.
Paperback: 978-1-84694-803-9 ebook: 978-1-84694-804-6

Wild Earth, Wild Soul
A Manual for an Ecstatic Culture
Bill Pfeiffer
Imagine a nature-based culture so alive and so connected, spreading like wildfire. This book is the first flame...
Paperback: 978-1-78099-187-0 ebook: 978-1-78099-188-7

Naming the Goddess
Trevor Greenfield
Naming the Goddess is written by over eighty adherents and scholars of Goddess and Goddess Spirituality.
Paperback: 978-1-78279-476-9 ebook: 978-1-78279-475-2

Shapeshifting into Higher Consciousness
Heal and Transform Yourself and Our World with Ancient
Shamanic and Modern Methods
Llyn Roberts
Ancient and modern methods that you can use every day
to transform yourself and make a positive difference in the
world.
Paperback: 978-1-84694-843-5 ebook: 978-1-84694-844-2

Readers of ebooks can buy or view any of these bestsellers by
clicking on the live link in the title. Most titles are published
in paperback and as an ebook. Paperbacks are available in
traditional bookshops. Both print and ebook formats are
available online.

Find more titles and sign up to our readers' newsletter at http://
www.johnhuntpublishing.com/paganism
Follow us on Facebook at https://www.facebook.com/
MoonBooks
and Twitter at https://twitter.com/MoonBooksJHP